FLANNERY O'CONNOR

A MEMORIAL

FLANNERY O'CONNOR

A MEMORIAL

Edited by

JOHN J. QUINN, S.J.

Scranton: University of Scranton Press

Reprinted 1996

University of Scranton Press
Editorial Office:
Linden and Monroe
Scranton PA 18510

University of Scranton Press
Business Office

Library of Congress Catalog Number 94-061556
ISBN 0-940866-42-0 HC
ISBN 0-940866-43-9 PB

Quinn, John J., Editor
Flannery O'Connor: A Memorial/John J. Quinn
Includes Index

Marketing and Distribution

University of Scranton Press
Chicago Distribution Center
11030 S. Langley
Chicago IL 60628

PRINTED IN THE UNITED STATES OF AMERICA

This book is dedicated

to the memory of my parents

Dr. and Mrs. John J. Quinn

and

Flannery

TABLE OF CONTENTS

ACKNOWLEDGEMENTS

Thanks to Paul Lowry for his portrait of Flannery O'Connor and to Flannery's Mother for helping him to refine it until she was satisfied that it was an accurate protrayal.

Flannery's letter and her essay "The Regional Writer" are reproduced with the permission of Farrar, Straus and Giroux, Inc.

A special thanks to Robert V. Prislupsky who patiently and generously computerized the entire manuscript.

My deep gratitude to the late Rev. William F. Lynch, S.J., for his superb book *CHRIST and APOLLO* and his invaluable assistance.

Thanks to Prof. Erick Mottram, my mentor at King's College, University of London, for helping me "see" Flannery.

PUBLISHER'S PREFACE

In the late 50's the University of Scranton in Pennsylvania established a small campus journal "Of Thought and Opinion" called *ESPRIT*. Its first Faculty Moderator was Fr John J. Quinn, S.J., a member of the English Department. For some time he had been working on and with the American writer Flannery O'Connor, even visiting with her mother on their farm in Georgia. When she died young in 1964 of a gradual disease, he conceived the idea of issuing a commemorative edition of *ESPRIT* in her honor (Vol 8 Winter 1964. No 1) and set about soliciting and receiving a large number of very kind and thoughtful tributes to Flannery the person and the writer. These included brief notes and extended critical remarks from a number of the outstanding literary figures in America at the time. When edited and completed with some background essays and a letter to Fr Quinn from Flannery and a recent essay of hers, it added up to a remarkable volume. Somewhat to the surprise of Fr Quinn and the staff of *ESPRIT*, there was a heavy demand from around the country for copies of this special edition, a demand that continued for some years afterwards until the entire stock was depleted.

Since 1994 is the 30th anniversary of her death, Fr Quinn now Professor Emeritus in the English Department, thought that it was time to reissue this tribute containing as it does what have now become historically important comments by important American literary figures. The University of Scranton Press therefore is happy to bring this process full circle by reprinting the original text while adding to it at the end a brief section of updating material.

PROLOGUE

ESPRIT is singularly honored in its association with Miss Flannery O'Connor.

From its first faltering steps to its present stance as an All American College Magazine, *ESPRIT* has had the good fortune of having the interest, encouragement, and guidance of this superb American Writer.

Miss O'Connor has made invaluable suggestions and contributions to *ESPRIT*. She judged its first Short Story Contest; she also enhanced it by appearing in its Short Story Symposium (Winter 1959-III-I) and publishing an illuminating article, first seen in print here, "The Regional Writer," (Winter 1963-VII-I).

With therefore, justifiable pride, *ESPRIT* dedicates this special memorial edition to her and gratefully acknowledges its indebtedness to the many famous people who join our tribute to a lovely lady and great literary artist. In so honoring us by honoring her, they also, we feel, honor themselves.

ESPRIT is also pleased publicly to thank Mrs. Edward F. O'Connor and her charming family for the gracious hospitality extended *ESPRIT* on the occasion of its unforgettable weekend (October 30-November 2, 1964) visit to Andalusia, the O'Connor Farm outside Milledgeville, Georgia.

FOREWORD

FLANNERY O'CONNOR'S 'COUNTRY'

J. J. QUINN, S.J.

To trace the lines in the topography of Flannery O'Connor's 'country' is to draw the human heart.

The network of veins and the highways of arteries chart the human condition on this map of Modern Man in his "personalistic universe," his "*Noosphere*," the sphere of mind and spirit, his "Socialization," that is, concern with the development of individuals as persons and with society on the level of interpersonal relationships — to use the terms of her favorite scientist-philosopher, Pierre Teilhard de Chardin, S.J.

Thus, it demands the eagle eyes of a stout Cortez to stare at this country and an unblinking honesty in travelers to look at its inhabitants with a wild surmise, or they reflect the very images of the travelers.

FLANNERY O'CONNOR

Travelers are discoverers, like it or no. They are wayfarers who need a compass; pioneers who need a leader with vision, courage, skill, and spirit. Lacking these, they are confusedly lost in the vertiginous maze of life's lines. The longitude of Hope and the latitude of Charity become enmeshed in the skeins of Fate, False Philosophies, and Foul Fickleness to tie Faith in a knot and Man in a bind of isolation. The thread of circumstance becomes the enslaving chain of habit; the challenge to personal enrichment by way of love becomes, not an adventure, but a soap opera; the call to greatness — to human and social fulfillment — blurs into the empty echo of a commercial.

Silent, upon a farm outside Milledgeville, Georgia, still the voice, sounding very like John the Baptist's, rings clear in two novels and two collections of short stories. The country is terribly, clearly delineated from its Scriptural lines out of the West's Judaeo-Christian tradition to its fictional contours of the deep South. The terrain traversed is frighteningly familiar; the accent may be southern but the voice is Man's own; the Oedipal search belongs to the reader himself, the search to channel his personal love, "the fundamental energy of life" (Teilhard), into the mainstream of Society's inter-personal communion.

"*Does one's integrity ever lie in what he is not able to do?*" Miss O'Connor asks in her introduction to *Wise Blood*, reissued ten years after its initial appearance. Her answer: "*I think that usually it does, for free will does not mean one will, but many wills conflicting in one man. Freedom cannot be conceived simply. It is a mystery and one which a novel, even a comic novel, can only be asked to deepen.*"

Mystery is reverentially respected — kept intact; but the tension problem of Man: his puzzling existence — *Am I?*, his anguished searching — *Who am I?*, absurd resistance — *Dare I?*, anxious commitment — *Should I?*, torturous *engagement* — *Must I?* through Life's plunging valleys and exhausting hills and turbulent waters and perilous wastelands is graphically surveyed by this writer of prophetic stature and vocation whose literary macrocosm is Man's microcosm.

FOREWORD

As did Teilhard in his scientific-philosophic findings discover "an inverse form of gravitation" — the ascent of life toward spirit and of spirit toward Omega is due to an attraction from above, namely, the divine, personal, transcendent Omega, "loving and loveable at this very moment," so does Flannery O'Connor reveal in her fictional upsidedown world Man's discovery of his awful power to embrace or reject Omega in his existentially free acceptance or free refusal to love. Like Teilhard, she firmly believed: "By virtue of the Creation, and still more, of the Incarnation, nothing here below is profane for those who know how to see" (The Divine Milieu p. 35).

This valiant lady — whose compass needle pointed unswervingly to the north star of Man's Redemption by Christ; whose unyielding vision of reality stripped the false label of 'natural' from the ugly rottenness of repugnant distortion to see life and Man as did King Lear, "The thing itself!" (and as Christ Himself, worth dying for!); whose personal courage under this staggering vision and artistic demands discerned an almost cosmic, ironically wry humor in our Human Comedy; whose literary skill and invincible spirit followed the lines of man from Lost to Regained Paradise only to discover the water of Baptism mingled with the blood of the Cross to direct lonely Man's way along History's Social Throughways to the profound human meaning of internal growth and Man's ever-threatened responsible freedom of interdependence, leading, not to "termite hill instead of brotherhood" (Teilhard's phrase), but to the liberty of unity in his complex day as he progresses to his destiny, homeward to his true country — this valiant lady is the song we sing.

Lest the Prophet be without honor in her own terrestrial country, *ESPRIT* heralds her enriching contribution to modern literature, salutes her own remarkably violent spirit that bears away the Kingdom of Heaven, and pays tribute to FLANNERY O'CONNOR.

The Achievement
of
Flannery O'Connor

John Clarke
University of Scranton

In the untimely death of Flannery O'Connor America has lost a fiction writer of rich talent and unusual perspective before her considerable promise could be fulfilled. The vision of reality which underlies her work seems strangely out of harmony with our materialistic, essentially non-religious society. Even among those who share her stark outlook on life there probably will be continued disagreement over the merits of the bizarre, often terrifying stories through which her concepts found artistic expression. Is her view of the contemporary world that which any true Christian eventually must assume? Or, as has been charged, is her fiction "gratuitously grotesque," indulging needlessly in violence and garish circumstances for their shock values? The attitude which one ultimately adopts toward Miss O'Connor's fiction probably will hinge upon the reader's religious and artistic inclinations, but even her sternest critics will readily concede that she was a compelling and challenging writer. Indeed, her powers of imagination were sometimes nothing short of awesome.

Miss O'Connor's total literary output was not extraordinarily large, even for one who died at the premature age of thirty-nine. Her short stories first began to appear after World War II in such prestige magazines as *Kenyon Review, Partisan Review* and *Accent*. In 1952 her first novel was published, *Wise Blood*, four of whose fourteen chapters previously had appeared separately. A collection of ten short stories, *A Good Man Is Hard to Find*, was published in 1955. Her second novel, *The Violent Bear It Away* (1960), received widespread favorable comment and is generally regarded as her best work. Other short stories have appeared periodically in the previously mentioned magazines, as well as in *Sewanee Review, Mademoiselle* and *Harper's Bazaar*. It is reported that a second collection of short stories is to be published posthumously in February, 1965, under the title of *Everything That Rises Must Converge*, a line taken from the writings of the late Jesuit philosopher Pierre Teilhard de Chardin. Supplementing her fiction are various critical observations she offered in articles that appeared in *America*; in a 1957 symposium entitled *The Living Novel*; in remarks before the Georgia Writers' Association which were reprinted in *Esprit*, and in several other interviews and panel discussions. If collected and analyzed, these critical comments would help to clarify Miss O'Connor's fictional practices, which have seemed so extravagant to some. Despite contentions to the contrary, there is a remarkable consistency between her theory and her practice. Finally, there is an off-beat article by Miss O'Connor in Holiday magazine for September, 1961, which deals with her hobby of raising peafowl and which, curiously, also helps to explain her perspectives on life and literature.

Certain paradoxes about Miss O'Connor's literary career cannot escape notice. She wrote under some severe physical handicaps, suffering from a bone ailment which eventually proved fatal and which made it necessary for her to use crutches during the last eight years of her life. As a Catholic, she was a member of a small minority in her native Georgia. Although her stories are Southern to the core, she was never actively part of any Southern literary movement and, for the most part, her fiction does not reflect the social issues, particularly the racial problems, which beset the South during her lifetime. Despite her Catholic faith, the characters of the bulk of her fiction are Protestant Fundamentalists or fanatics. While her tales are so strikingly modern in conception as to be almost revolutionary, Miss O'Connor eschewed most modern literary methods. Her stories, for example, generally follow a strict chronological arrangement and contain neither stream-of-consciousness narration nor existentialist brooding upon the world's ills.

Her Stories

What they do contain is an astonishing and often appalling assortment of murderers, wild-eyed preachers, psychologically warped youngsters, charlatans, adulterers, perverts, ignorant rednecks and generally wretched heroes. Brutality, violence, mayhem, deceit, sardonic twists and the deaths of innocents are among the staples of her fiction. Her stories are seldom pleasant reading and, to the uninitiate, the sin and gore might seem pointless, nothing more than naturalism of the basest variety run utterly amok. But this, as will be seen, is to misread her fiction.

The title tale of Miss O'Connor's *Good Man* is typical of the sensationalism that glosses the surface of her art. The story opens almost jocularly with a Georgia family of five squabbling but without real rancor at the outset of a motor trip. The bantering is sprinkled with some ominous references to a criminal called The Misfit who has escaped from a penitentiary in the region. As the Bailey family drives along, the woolly-minded grandmother's ramblings about a haunted house infect the two small children who pester their father into taking a side excursion on a dirt road to see the old plantation. The car upsets in a gulch and The Misfit and two henchmen come upon the helpless group. The garrulous grandmother recognizes the fugitive and tells him so. Thereupon, one by one, all five members of the family are shot dead, the chatterbox grandmother last, after the cold-blooded Misfit has incredibly compared himself to Christ and complained that he "can't make what all I done wrong fit what all I gone through in punishment."

These shocking events must be understood against the backdrop of Miss O'Connor's over-all philosophic outlook if they are to be anything beyond sadistic. The story is in keeping with her literary conjuration of contemporary life, which she bluntly regarded as horrifying and grotesque. It was her conviction that modern man has lost contact with the essential scheme of Redemption. Men, she thought, are either lost in trivial, secular concerns (the Bailey family) or searching fanatically and ineffectually for the true paths of Grace, and often acting in diametric opposition to what is genuinely virtuous (The Misfit). The rock-bed of her belief was that the perspective on life of most of mankind had become so warped that it could be depicted only through grotesque symbols. Her approach, consequently, is basically negative in that she strives to make the reader aware of virtue's beauty by showing him the ugliness of its absence.

"Writers who see by the light of their Christian faith," she once declared, "will have, in these times the sharpest eyes for the grotesque, for the perverse and for the unacceptable. . . . The novelist with Christian concerns will find in modern life distortions which are repugnant to him, and his problem will be to make these appear as distortions to an audience which is used to seeing them as natural." The jarring and frightful world she portrayed was, she said, more real to her than that which most people regard as real. Conversely, the attitudes toward life which she witnessed around her were, she indicated, more grotesque than any of the characters she created. Her viewpoint is thus apocalyptic, piercing through the outward manifestations of life to an inner spiritual turmoil. In this chaos, of which her fictional creations were symbols, confused and misshapen souls are groping blindly, some in vain pursuit of spurious earthly goals and others in furious, even blasphemous search for meaning to life. In the Blakean universe she presents, Miss O'Connor's sympathies were clearly aligned with the mistaken Truth-Seekers, the raging, irrational, even sinful prophets, some of whom seem to have wandered into the modern world from the pages of the Old Testament. They at least have some awareness of reality, some cognizance of the Divine Plan, she contended. They may reject or pervert The Word but they cannot escape it. On the other hand, Miss O'Connor's utmost scorn was showered upon the secularists, bogged in their material world and unable or unwilling to perceive the grand design of existence, the plan of Redemption.

For Miss O'Connor, therefore, even Hazel Motes, the half-crazed hero of *Wise Blood*, has certain commendable qualities despite his lechery, his sadism, his horrible act of self-immolation in burning out his eyes with quicklime. Although he wallows in sin and thunders incoherently and futilely on behalf of his new "Church Without Christ," perverting almost all the natural aims of religion, he is superior to that mundane life which ignores God and is concerned only with the pursuit of temporal happiness. Such an existence, Flannery O'Connor felt, was more weird and distorted than the most outlandish of Hazel Motes' actions. This is perhaps why, at the close of the novel, the spent and dying Motes is seen by his worldly, uncomprehending landlady as "going backwards to Bethlehem." For him there is at least some hope of Redemption.

A Sacred Rage

Miss O'Connor's transcendent views are ordered most explicitly in *The Violent Bear It Away*, a haunting account of a fourteen-year-old-boy-prophet named Tarwater who, like so many of our heroes, feels obliged to accomplish a mission in life. Reared in the backwoods by his fiery, fanatical, Bible-quoting great uncle, Old Tarwater, the youth has been reminded repeatedly that he must, first, give the old man a decent burial when he dies, and, second, baptize the idiot son of his city-dwelling uncle, Rayber, who is a schoolteacher and a psychologist. When the old man dies, however, the Devil persuades Tarwater to neglect his first duty. Instead, he burns down the farmhouse with the old man's body inside and goes to the city where he eventually is taken into Rayber's home. What is involved at the heart of the novel is a contest for the boy's soul, torn by the teachings of the old, mad and now dead great uncle and those of his atheistic schoolteacher-uncle. Both combatants are essentially grotesques in Miss O'Connor's view, but she regarded the godless outlook of the scientifically-oriented schoolteacher as the more impaired.

The divergent views of Old Tarwater and Rayber are crystallized in their attitudes toward the retarded child, Bishop. To the self-styled prophet, the child remains "precious in the sight of the Lord." To the secularized schoolteacher, his idiot son is merely "a mistake of nature," a mistake which he once attempted to correct by drowning the boy, only to find himself inexplicably restrained by an overwhelming sense of love.

In the end, young Tarwater proves a disciple of his ranting

great uncle. He baptizes Bishop and, in an appalling touch of irony, drowns the child in the process. After some additional encounters with the secular world that leave him further scarred, Tarwater, bent on a career as prophet, sets his face "toward the dark city, where the children of God lay sleeping," and presumably a fate similar to that of Hazel Motes.

Seen as Flannery O'Connor intended it to be seen, *The Violent Bear It Away* is a shocking indictment of the present world for its lack of true spirituality. Young Tarwater is a monster and Rayber is even worse because they move in a shadowy realm outside the true scheme of Redemption. Of the two, Miss O'Connor indicated, Tarwater with his prophetic violent view of reality is preferable, even more comprehensible. This is the significance of the novel's title, taken from Matthew 11:12 (interestingly, the King James version), in which Christ declares that "from the days of John the Baptist, the kingdom of heaven suffereth violence and the violent bear it away." What Flannery O'Connor implied was that some sacred rage, some enthusiasm such as that roused by John for the new Gospel, can give man a faint glimpse of the reality from which he has strayed. Until men are fully in accord with the divine teleology, however, life will be the grotesque and sinful thing mirrored in her novel.

Aspects of her Art

To concentrate exclusively on Miss O'Connor's complex symbolism, however, is to slight other aspects of her considerable art. These would include her brilliant sense of irony, her command of cracker-barrel jargon, her ability to make her characters come alive, even those who seem eccentric beyond belief. Few other writers could even fashion a story about so bizarre a figure as Joy Hopewell of the short story "Good Country People," an embittered, thirty-two-year-old blonde with a wooden leg and a Ph.D. in philosophy, who has changed her name to Hulga and who dreams of seducing a bumptious young Bible salesman.

Miss O'Connor had a particular knack for the pithy simile. In *The Life You Save May Be Your Own*, for example, one finds this gripping sentence: "The ugly words settled in Mr. Shiftlet's head like a group of buzzards in the top of a tree." Enoch Emery of *Wise Blood* tells Hazel Motes about the woman with whom he had once lived whose "hair was so thin it looked like ham gravy trickling over her skull." As Haze bends over a mummy case elsewhere in the novel, his eyes are "like two clean bullet holes." Opposite him, the faces of two little boys beside their snickering mother are "like pans set on either side to catch the grins that overflowed from her." The young wife in "A Good Man" has a face "as broad and innocent as a cabbage," and a little later the doomed, prattling grandmother raises her head "like a parched old turkey hen crying for water." Similar, country-fresh similes can be found in almost every story Flannery O'Connor wrote.

Often in a single sentence Miss O'Connor was able to capture the essence of a character: "Besides the neutral expression that she wore when she was alone, Mrs. Freeman had two others, forward and reverse, that she used for all her human dealings." ("Good Country People"). Having lived most of her life in a farmhouse at Milledgeville, Georgia, Miss O'Connor had a remarkable ability to reproduce Southern dialect. Both Tarwaters like to snap, "That's my bidnis" for "business," and Enoch Emery's talk is sprinkled with such colloquial slang as "thetere" (that there), "thiseyer" (this here), and "sommers" (somewhere) .

What is frequently referred to as grim humor in Miss O'Connor's writings is more probably irony. A thorough study of the matter would be a worthwhile contribution to literary scholarship. If her stories are amusing in any sense, they assuredly are ferocious comedies. At any rate, elements of the ludicrous can be found in many passages, of which the following, from *Wise Blood*, might be typical:

> ... Haze had driven his car immediately to the nearest garage where a man with black bangs and a short expressionless face had come out to wait on him. He told the man he wanted the horn made to blow and the leaks taken out of the gas tank, the starter made to work smoother and the windshield wipers tightened.
>
> The man lifted the hood and glanced inside and then shut it again. Then he walked around the car, stopping to lean on it here and there, and thumping it in one place and another. Haze asked

him how long it would take to put it in the best order. "It can't be done," the man said.

"This is a good car," Haze said. "I knew when I first saw it that it was the car for me, and since I've had it, I've had a place to be that I can always get away in."

"Was you going some place in this ? "the man asked.

"To another garage," Haze said, and he got in the Essex and drove off. At the other garage he went to, there was a man who said he could put the car in the best shape overnight, because it was such a good car to begin with, so well put together and with such good materials in it, and because, he added, he was the best mechanic in town, working in the best-equipped shop. Haze left it with him, certain that it was in honest hands.

Similarly, there are both comic and pathetic qualities to Miss O'Connor's description of young Tarwater's first visit to the city in *The Violent Bear It Away*, a section which also illustrates the author's penetrating insight into the naive mind of a rustic youngster:

... On the way from the railroad station he had walked tall in the mass of moving metal and concrete speckled with the very small eyes of people. The glitter of his own eyes was shaded under the stiff roof-like brim of a new grey hat balanced perfectly straight on his buttressing ears. Before coming he had read facts in the almanac and he knew that there were 75,000 people here who were seeing him for the first time. He wanted to stop and shake hands with each of them and say his name was F. M. Tarwater and that he was here only for the day to accompany his uncle on business at a lawyers. His head jerked backwards after each passing figure until they began to pass too thickly and he observed that their eyes didn't grab at you like the eyes of country people. Several people bumped into him and this contact that should have made an acquaintance for life, made nothing because the hulks shoved on with ducked heads and muttered apologies that he would have accepted if they had waited.

It is, of course, still too soon to define Flannery O'Connor's position in American and world literature, but some literary relationships can be traced. As a Catholic writer she has been compared to the early Graham Greene, and as a Southerner she bears some obvious indebtedness to William Faulkner. Her literary style is markedly unlike Faulkner's and her characters inhabit no earthly Yoknapatawpha County, but some kinship is evident between her callous, ranting rednecks and his Snopses. Similarities have been noted specifically between some of her characters and the Bundrens of *As I Lay Dying*.

The grotesque manner of Miss O'Connor's fiction is not new to our literature. The tradition extends back through Sherwood Anderson and Ambrose Bierce to Edgar Allan Poe and even Washington Irving. Some of Miss O'Connor's contemporaries, second generation writers of the Southern Renaissance such as Truman Capote and Carson McCullers, also have dealt in grotesques, although it is highly doubtful that their motivations are religious like Miss O'Connor's. It would be unfair, however, to link Flannery O'Connor too closely with any Southern movement. As a recent commentator noted, in her technique of the completely removed author and her cold, hard phrases, she really resembles Stephen Crane and Hemingway more than the typical Southern author.

Perhaps on firmer grounds, Miss O'Connor has been compared with the American surrealistic novelist Nathanael West, who, by coincidence, also died in his late thirties, probably before his talents had fully matured. Despite their differences in religious temperament, both writers had a horror of sentimentality and both decried the image of man as a creature whose rationality made him self-sufficient. Diabolical figures, if not the Devil himself, appear in both of their fiction.

Flannery O'Connor preferred to think of herself as an author in the tradition of Hawthorne, "though I hope with less reliance on allegory." There is much to support this critical judgment of her own talents. Like Miss O'Connor, Hawthorne was concerned with man's relation to sin and evil. He too viewed the world as a façade behind which spiritual forces for good and bad were locked in titanic struggle. For Hawthorne, as for Miss O'Connor, man was essentially a fallen creature, capable of dark sin. Both writers distrusted logic and the heartless, scientific approach as tools for unraveling the truths of the cosmos. Hawthorne's Ethan Brand is a grotesque in the O'Connor vein, and the tragic vision of young Goodman Brown is not altogether unlike that of Hazel Motes. What Caroline Gordon once said of Miss O'Connor's characters is equally applicable to many of Hawthorne's: "They are lost in that abyss which opens for man when he sets up as God."

The South, specifically the evangelistic, rural South, gave Miss O'Connor the materials of her stories, but the vision that infused them was that of her Catholic faith. If the synthesis surprises us, it may be because we have had too narrow a notion of what Catholic literature might embrace. Miss O'Connor has expanded our view, even if it should be the verdict of time that the sensational situations of her stories transgress artistic limits. In the persisting paucity in America of Catholics who are good fiction writers, her absence will be sorely felt. Flannery O'Connor's greatest accomplishment may have been to demonstrate that religion, far from being a barrier to art, should be its vital center. That is the essence of a comment she once made which some undiscerning critics have thought mere tautology: "When people have told me that because I am a Catholic, I cannot be an artist, I have had to reply, ruefully, that because I am a Catholic I cannot afford to be less than an artist."

Biography

1925   March 25
   Mary FLANNERY was born to Edward Francis and Regina
   Cline O'Connor: Savannah, Georgia.

1937-41 Peabody High School and
1941-45 Woman's College of Georgia: Milledgeville, Georgia.
   (B. A. - Social Science)

1945-47 Writer's Workshop, University of Iowa (Master of Fine Arts)

1946   "The Geranium," *Accent*, 6, Summer, 1946: first published story.

1952   WISE BLOOD, first novel. Harcourt, Brace & Co., New York.

1953   "The Life You Save May Be Your Own," *Prize Stories 1954:
   The O. Henry Awards.* Garden City, 1954.

1954   "A Circle in the Fire," *Prize Stories 1955: The O. Henry Awards.*
   Second Prize Story. *The Best American Short Stories of 1955.*
   Boston, 1955.

1954-5 Fellowship in Fiction, *Kenyon Review.*

1955   A GOOD MAN IS HARD TO FIND, first collection of Short Stories.
   Harcourt, Brace & Co. "The Artificial Nigger," *The Best American
   Short Stories of 1956.*

1956   "Greenleaf," First Prize Story, *Prize Stories 1957: The O. Henry
   Awards.* Also included in: *The Best American Short Stories of 1957*
   and *First Prize Stories, 1919-1957,* the O. Henry Memorial Awards.

1957   "A View of the Woods," *The Best American Short Stories of 1958.*
   Grant from the National Academy of Arts and Letters.

1959 $10,000 Grant from the Ford Foundation.

1960   THE VIOLENT BEAR IT AWAY, Novel. Farrar, Straus and Cudahy, N.Y.

1962   "Everything That Rises Must Converge," *The Best American Short
   Stories of 1962.* Reissue WISE BLOOD.

1963   "Everything That Rises Must Converge." First Prize Story, *Prize
   Stories 1963: The O. Henry Awards.*

1964   August 3 R. I. P.

1965   January, Tribute to Flannery O'Connor: ESPRIT. April, EVERYTHING
   THAT RISES MUST CONVERGE, last collection of short stories.
   Farrar, Straus and Giroux, New York.

A TRIBUTE to
Flannery O'Connor

A TRIBUTE
TO
FLANNERY
O'CONNOR

Walter Allen
Critic, Writer: London

Flannery O'Conner was certainly the finest writer the American South has produced since Carson McCullers, and to the reader who knows the South only through its literature, she must have seemed quintessentially of the South. That she was conscious of this herself seems plain from the essay she wrote called "The Fiction Writer and His Country," in which she speaks of the "Southern school" as conjuring up "an image of Gothic monstrosities and the idea of a preoccupation with everything deformed and grotesque. Most of us are considered, I believe, to be unhappy combinations of Poe and Erskine Caldwell."

But if her "Southernness" is her first obvious quality, it is equally obvious she is using what might be called her Southern properties with a difference; so much so that in the end her "Southernness" becomes, in one sense, the least important aspect of her. Like Faulkner and Mrs. McCullers at their best, she utterly transcends her locale; or rather, through the local she attains the universal. For she was nothing if not a religious novelist and story-writer, which is something quite different from being — as she was not — a propagandist in fiction for her own religious faith. In fact, though I am not myself a Catholic, I do not think that what she did could have been done, in a Southern context, by any writer except a Catholic; but what she worked in terms of, all the time, was the familiar religious situation of the South, the situation of what one is tempted to call Protestant primitivism.

This fact of primitivism is important. What she describes is a world of the God-intoxicated; indeed, in *The Violent Bear It Away* the world outside the God-intoxicated scarcely exists at all, and the atheist Rayber, for instance, is, for all his repudiation of God, is shown as really as much intoxicated by God as Francis Marion Tarwater and the prophet, his great-uncle.

In a note she appended in 1962 to a new edition of *Wise Blood*, she said: "The book was written with zest and, if possible, it should be read that way. It is a comic novel about a Christian *malgre lui*, and as such, very serious, for all comic novels that are any good must be about matters of life and death." She wrote, one feels, always with zest; the reader is carried along at a furious pace. And she was a remarkable comic writer; I can think of no one like her. She was, I feel, something of a Primitive herself, as comes out in her remark about her work: "It is literal in the same sense that a child's drawing is literal." She added: "I am interested in the lines that create spiritual motion." Create it she did, in all its power, its apparent crudeness and savage violence.

There is often a considerable time-lag before a writer on one side of the Atlantic receives proper recognition on the other. This was true in Flannery O'Connor's case: in England my guess is that her work was almost unknown outside Catholic circles. That England will catch up with her eventually, as it did however belatedly with Nathanael West, I don't doubt. Just as I don't doubt that her untimely death represented a loss that is quite incalculable to American writing.

Brother Antoninus, O. P.
   Poet

Flannery O'Connor was unique among American Catholic

writers in that she did not deflect from the problem of violence that is the central preoccupation of our literature. We have produced many able poets and fictionists who have accommodated the uses of irony and mordant insight that our time has perfected, but none like Flannery O'Connor who brought those elements to bear upon the problem of violence itself. Her classicism did not soften her gaze. Rather, it provided the medium through which her gaze could penetrate to the essentiality of what she sought. Doubtless the facts of her personal life enabled her to confront the problem of violence in the search for understanding. I do not know what they were, but there was in her work an affinity to the humanity of her characters that could only have come from deep interior suffering. At the same time the sharp intellectual dryness insured her situation in the twentieth century literary scene. I do not feel that she left a great work undone. I feel that she accomplished in full measure what she was sent to do. It is my hope that other Catholic writers will not fear the fascination with violence that is the essence of American literature, but will develop the heart, as she did, to take that violence to its only point of solution: the cross.

Saul Bellow
Novelist

I was distressed to hear of Miss O'Connor's death. I admire her books greatly and had the same feeling for the person who wrote them. I wish I were able to say more, but it isn't possible just now.

Sr. Bertrande (Meyers), D. C.
Writer, Pres. Merillac College, Mo.

Flannery O'Connor was denied the biblical life of three score and ten, actually missing two score by one short year. In number, her writings matched her years in fewness. Two novels, one collection of short stories, another collection to be published posthumously, make up the sum total of her contribution to the contemporary literary world. Yet, for some fourteen of her thirty-nine years, Flannery O'Connor was a figure in that world — not a predominant figure, but one whose prominence was heightened by the controversial opinions aroused by her writings. Her proven potentialities as a writer insured that she would be kept in mind; by some, hopefully, and by others, uneasily.

For Flannery O'Connor had her fans and her foes, not in equal numbers. Her admirers, I believe, far outnumbered her adversaries; at least her admirers were more articulate, although her foes, when vocal, were almost vituperatively so. To both she was a sign and a symbol just as an anchor, a flag, a cross or a caduceus is a sign. In reviewing her life and works one cannot escape the fact that Flannery was "set for a sign that shall be contradicted" and contradictions there were aplenty. But of what was she a sign? Aye, there's the rub, for neither her admirers or her adversaries seem sure of just what her symbolism signified. Hostile critics coined such alliterative epithets as "ferocious Flannery" and accused her of deliberately cultivating the "gratuitously grotesque" in the selection of her dramatis personae. Her admirers, with definite certainty of their admiration, but somewhat unsure of just what they admired, wrote of her perceptive skill in character delineation, of her psychological insights and her ability to face stark reality and appraise it for what it was. But most of all they applauded her creative capacity to see teeming life with its inevitable tragedy in the apparently drab, commonplace, unchallenging detail of everyday life without losing an iota of her unfailing compassion for all that is human, however erring. Actually, however, both foe and friend missed the point and purpose of Flannery O'Connor's "message" until she herself supplied the key.

Ways of Interpretation

There are two ways of interpreting an author's meaning: one is to see and understand the author — and the message he is attempting to convey — through his writings and what they reveal. The other is to interpret the writings after coming to know the author, either by personal contact or by reading what he has to say of himself. I have an idea that Flannery would have preferred the former method for she indeed recognized the curious fact that up until mid-1957 all critics, favorable and unfavorable of Flannery O'Connor, seemed to be saying the same thing. There isn't space to go into this, but there seemed to be an uncertainty, a vagueness and, at best, a reserved appreciation of Flannery's "perceptiveness" and an acceptance of the fact that she was skilled in drawing unusual portraits of unusual characters. This came from those who favored the author. From those who did not there were all sorts of accusations about her penchant for freaks, her refusal to deal with Catholic themes or characters, and that she seemed to revel in presenting immoral situations and amoral people for no apparent moral purpose.

Even admirers of Flannery's stories seemed somehow unsure of what point she was making, and neither friend nor foe seemed able or willing to really take her stories apart and analyze them to the satisfaction of the curious, puzzled reader. Critics described the stories, retold them in other words, but somehow they seemed unable to cope with the pattern or point up the purpose. This was frustrating to certain fan-readers, not given to writing, for they felt that decoded and deciphered her stories had something very real and very Catholic and very ecumenical about them—something very fundamental to faith. Actually, Flannery came to grips with the Incarnation, to the essence of religion, the fact that Christ died for all men. It helped a great deal if the reader knew his Bible.

Then, almost as if constrained to do so, Flannery spoke up for herself. In her chapter, "The Fiction Writer and His Country," a contribution to Granville Hicks' symposium, *The Living Novel* (published by Macmillan in 1957), Flannery clearly states the purpose of her writing. In seven pages of unassailable logic and uncompromising phrases, written in her own cogent style, with its seasoned sarcasm, biting irony, and saving humor, Flannery brings into sharp focus the import of her fiction: "I am no disbeliever in spiritual purpose," she says, "and I am no vague believer. I see from the standpoint of Christian orthodoxy. This means for me the meaning of life is centered in our Redemption by Christ and that what I see in the world I see in its relation to that." She added, not as an afterthought, but out of her experience of being so often misinterpreted, "I don't think that this is a position that can be taken halfway or one that is particularly easy in these times to make transparent in fiction."

Writing is a Vocation

For her friends and for all who wrote fairly of her, this statement was taken at face value and used as a sort of Rosetta Stone after 1957. A spate of articles followed with titles to prove this acceptance and to disprove her earlier critics: "Flannery O'Connor and the Reality of Sin" (*Catholic World*, January 1959) "Flannery O'Connor's Way: Shock with Moral Intent" (*Renascence*, Summer 1963) "Fact and Mystery: Flannery O'Connor" (*Commonweal*, December 6, 1963). For that matter, this writer herself followed what might be termed the party line — a good line it was, and true — "Four Stories of Flannery O'Connor" (*Commonweal*, Autumn 1962). But we all missed something vital; something that Flannery told us so plainly: that the ability to write is not only a gift from God but a vocation, and "a vocation," she says, "is a limiting factor which extends even to the kind of material that the writer is able to apprehend imaginatively." The point she was making is that a writer may choose what he will write about but he cannot choose what he is able to make come alive. And herein lies the factor that made so many critics stumble. Vocation is not an easy thing to understand. Someday when space is not a problem this writer would like to study Flannery in light of her God-given vocation. I would wish that I might have done this while she was living, for Flannery and I came to be friends, and once she turned to me at a time she was deeply and grossly misunderstood — and calumniated ....

But now Flannery is gone. What is written is written. Even as Yahweh "raised the needy from the dust and lifted up the poor man from the dunghill" so did Flannery's creative genius, through her own sense of vocation, take the hard baked red clay of her native Georgia to make of it minor literary immortals. In discussing the constant accusation that she was preoccupied with the grotesque, the freaks of human nature rather than normal people, Flannery said earnestly, "Sister, I write about grotesque people because I write about them best. It is my vocation to write about Redemption, and when one sees life from that viewpoint one sees so many distortions in today's world that are accepted as normal and natural. To people who so accept distortions (as natural and normal) you have to exaggerate your point."

Flannery O'Connor was not an easy person to draw into protracted conversation about her work. But once I saw her face light up with an inner radiance, almost, one would say with the joy of discovery. We were discussing Tarwater in particular, and in general, why *The Violent Bear It Away* was not as successful as some of her stories. "They didn't understand it," I said, "they did not get the point. They were too concerned with details...." This was when her face lighted up. "But oh, I have had my complete fulfillment today," she said. "One of the young Sisters here at Merillac College told me that she 'read Tarwater loud and clear: I understand him perfectly! He was struggling with his vocation. I've been through that — I know just how he felt and you did, too." Pensive for a moment, Flannery smiled at me: "You couldn't ask more from any reader than that, now could you?"

Elizabeth Bishop
  Poet

I never met Flannery O'Connor, but we had been exchanging occasional letters for the last eight years or so. She invited me to visit her at "Andalusia" in Milledgeville, and how deeply I regret now that I never did. The closest I got to it was once when a freighter I was traveling on to South America put into Savannah for overnight. Wandering through those dusty, fusty little squares, I suddenly realized I was in Flannery O'Connor country and thought perhaps I could get to see her. I put in a telephone call from the booth in the lobby of the largest hotel; I remember that while I waited I studied a display of pecans and of boxes of "Miss Sadie's Bourbon Balls" on the candy and cigar counter just outside the booth. Quite soon a very collected, very Southern voice answered and immediately invited me to "come on over." Alas, the bus connections didn't work out so that I could get back to my freighter in time to sail.

Later she sent me some colored snapshots of herself, some with her peacocks, some of her alone, always on crutches. In these amateur snapshots she looks, in spite of the crutches, younger than her age and very much alive. From Brazil I sent her a cross in a bottle, like a ship in a bottle, crudely carved, with all the instruments of the Passion, the ladder, pliers, dice, etc., in wood, paper, and tinfoil, with the little rooster at the top of the cross. I thought it was the kind of innocent religious grotesquery she might like, and I think she did, because she wrote:

> If I were mobile and limber and rich I would come to Brazil at once after one look at this bottle. Did you observe that the rooster has an eyebrow? I particularly like him and the altar cloth a little dirty from the fingers of whoever cut it out . . . I am altogether taken with it. It's what I'm born to appreciate.

I feel great remorse now that I hadn't written to her for many months, that I had allowed this friendship to dwindle just when she must have been aware she was dying. Something about her intimidated me a bit: perhaps natural awe before her toughness and courage; perhaps, although death is certain for all, hers seemed a little more certain than usual. She made no show of not living in a metropolis, or of being a believer; she lived with Christian stoicism and wonderful wit and humor that put most of us to shame.

I am very glad to hear that another collection of her stories is to be published soon. I am sure her few books will live on and on in American literature. They are narrow, possibly, but they are clear, hard, vivid, and full of bits of description, phrases, and an odd insight that contains more real poetry than a dozen books of poems. Critics who accuse her of exaggeration are quite wrong, I think. I lived in Florida for several years next to a flourishing "Church of God" (both white and black congregation), where every Wednesday night Sister Mary and her husband "spoke in tongues." After those Wednesday nights, nothing Flannery O'Connor ever wrote could seem at all exaggerated to me.

Kay Boyle
Fiction Writer

I grieve that the clear and poignant voice of Flannery O'Connor is now silent. We needed the sound of it, the work that was vehicle for it, the special perceptivity and quality of courage that made that voice essentially her own. She was at the beginning of her career; but that beginning was filled with a wealth of achievement of which any American writer, no matter what his age, might be deeply proud. I know that Flannery O'Connor's work, and her spirit, will illuminate the way for many who are setting out on that perilous journey which every writer undertakes. In the convictions, and the strength of language in which she has stated those convictions, others will find enduring courage. I can think of no accomplishment more to be envied than this.

Charles A. Brady
Critic, Writer, Prof. Canisius College, N.Y.

One of the biggest difficulties in assessing contemporary literary reputations is the tendency to praise an emerging writer for the wrong reasons. This happened to Flannery O'Connor at the outset of her tragically brief career; and she didn't like it at all. She was right, too, to resent her quite different inventions being classed with the Southern grotesques of Carson McCullers and Truman Capote. For, where their grotesques were Dickensian, hers were Dostoevskian with a classic sense of form. Moreover, her complaint against the Southern novel's being regarded simply as a *de rigueur* Gothic construct, a kind of Charles Addams decaying mansion of the morbid fancy was, at the very least, valid for the kind of book she wrote.

All this was in the beginning, of course. But, even at the end, her real originality continued to be misidentified in certain critical quarters. She, a Catholic, had become the laureate of Southern Protestantism precisely because, as a Catholic, and one of Irish extraction to boot, she could understand from inside the splendors as well as the savagery of Southern Puritanism. It was a living thing to her, not a mere piece of cultural anthropology, not an obscurantist survival from and throwback to a dark period in the American soul.

I remember describing her once as Faulkner's "youngest disciple" — and so she was, in part, anyway, since no Southern writer of her generation could escape from his brooding, powerful, garrulous spell. But Faulkner — even in *Light in August*, in *Absolom Absolom!*, where his religious perceptions are at their most sensitive — was writing a *critique* of Southern Calvinism. She wasn't — not dominantly, anyway, though it is now a critical truism to say that she was. A lesser genius than Faulkner, she identified herself, empathetically even more than sympathetically, with a living, breathing religious fact, not with a sociological entity. He dealt in "Christ-figures," on occasion. She, like her characters, was out for Christ.

Fourteen-year-old Tarwater, the hero of her extraordinary second novel with its, for her, archetypal title, *The Violent Bear It Away*, brings to a dramatic focus the sort of preoccupation that made Miss O'Connor's fiction *sui generis* in its day. Tarwater is Huck Finn faced with a different crisis of conscience from conniving in the escape of a Negro slave. (Her selective muse, incidentally, took very little part in this particular tragic action.) Should he or should he not accept his dead great-uncle's laying on of hands and baptize the idiot son of his only blood relative, Uncle Rayber, who tries to free the boy from what he considers a destructive religious compulsion? The resultant struggle has a quality of comic epic about it cutting across the plane of her vernacular Divine Comedy. The reader finds himself smiling wryly as he, too, wrestles with the angel in his effort to resolve the dialectic young Tarwater encounters. Are children "cursed with believing?" Or, quite to the contrary, are children blessed for the very reason that their capacity for faith makes them citizens of the invisible country which must be finally taken by violence because it is the kingdom of heaven?

Miss O'Connor's harsh, violent art was partial to denouements of melodramatic violence. The iron ethic of her Georgian extension of Yoknapatawpha County would have been intolerable in its intensity if it had not been irradiated by a sense of compassion. As a sister under the skin of Bloy and Bernanos, her books did not realize the Beatitude which states that the meek inherit the earth. But the Christianity, which was the source of her deepest thematic compulsions, always poises on the needle point of violent paradox. In Flannery O'Connor's best writing it took the citadel of art by storm even as she, through it, one feels sure, has taken the kingdom of heaven.

Harvey Breit
Critic, Poet

We asked Miss O'Connor if she worked on her farm and she said quietly (but with quiet fervor), "No, I'm a writer." She told us she raised peacocks (some of them walk around in some of her stories), but we balked at asking her if she had a personal hand in it. She believes that what the writer needs the most is self-knowledge, that in knowing yourself you know everything, or nearly everything, about people. She doesn't think of herself as a Southern writer. "My people could come from anywhere," she told us, "but naturally since I know the South, they speak with a Southern accent." Which they do. They also speak with the simplicity of truth, and with its color and nuance.

(c) 1955 by "The N. Y. Times Co."(6/12/55). Reprinted by permission of writer and "Times."

Cleanth Brooks
Writer, Critic, Prof. Yale

I wish that time allowed me to write a considered tribute to the memory of Flannery O'Connor. It does not. Actually I saw and talked to Miss O'Connor on only one occasion. But the quality of her brave and dedicated spirit came through at once. In her instance, I find it hard to separate the person from the artist. Certainly the character of both was an invincible integrity.

This paragraph does not deserve appearing in your Memorial Edition, but I am very happy to know that you are doing such an edition and am happy to pay a personal tribute to this remark.

Oscar Cargill
Critic, Prof. New York University

Flannery O'Connor seems to have lost an important battle, but to have conducted herself more or less like St. George with the dragon. She did not wish to be known specifically as a "Southern" writer, half Erskine Caldwell and half Poe, in her own phrase, working with an impoverish background and a penchant for "Gothic" effects. She is a victim of facile labeling, one of the major critical vices in this country. I go along with her own conception of herself as a writer, not a red-clay Georgia writer, but just a writer, who reported faithfully the meagre life of her region and its obvious social decay, because these were the things her wide-angle lens took in. She would have seen them in Yonkers had it been her ill-fortune to have been born there, for all Westchester is not Bronxville, and not every Southern writer is William Faulkner or Carson McCullers, or wishes to be. Flannery O'Connor was herself, a highly skilled craftsman with a passion for accurate reporting and her skill put this achievement easily within her range.

Warren Coffey
    Critic, Prof. U. of San Francisco

Flannery O'Connor had the satirist's ear and the visionary's eye. Both are rare enough but rarer still the writer that has both. And it is the having both, I believe, which makes the Flannery O'Connor stories unique. They have a wholly admirable satiric art that freezes cliché as it falls and reveals the banality of a life or mind. And beyond and beneath the banality that the satirist can reach, Flannery O'Connor saw evil and got it flaming onto the pages of her books, evil a more mysterious thing altogether than banality and generally inaccessible to the satirist because it glimmers and crackles beneath the social surfaces that he by trade deals with. It takes the visionary's eyes to see evil, also — all Flannery O'Connor's books say — to see God. Having spoken of her books as *visionary*, one quickly adds that they are so only in the strict, literal sense of that word and that they regularly eschew dreaminess and easy swoons or raptures. If evil is always menacing in these books, God is always the God of the terrible encounter. Flannery O'Connor did not have three names, which is perhaps trivial to point out, but she never wrote like the ladies with three names, which is not. She stayed out of literary politics and went her own way down in Georgia. She was long intimate with pain and wrote always with death more or less in the next room. Few writers of the age have written as independently, fewer still with her bravery.

She knew her corner of Georgia and her people so well that she got them and our continent too and the world and time and race into some of the most original and brilliant stories of her generation. Two of these at least, *A Good Man is Hard to Find* and *Good Country People*, are likely to last as long as literacy. They seemed to me when I first read them some years ago and seem still today nearly perfect of their kind. Her novels suffer, I believe, from an excessive violence of conception, but one of them, *The Violent Bear It Away*, has sections of which it is impossible to deny the power and the strange beauty. We have all had a loss by the death of Flannery O'Connor.

Francis X. Connolly
Writer, Prof. Fordham University, N. Y.

In 1952 Robert Giroux, then an editor at Harcourt Brace, presented Flannery O'Connor's first novel, *Wise Blood*, to the American public. That public knew little of Flannery O'Connor, save that she came highly recommended by her editor and a few fastidious critics like Allen Tate. When I read *Wise Blood* I felt, without being able to formulate it, the spiritual thrust of Miss O'Connor's theme. She intended, as she put it in 1962, to write "a comic novel about a Christian *malgre lui*" and she explored a kind of negative integrity which was demonstrated not in what Hazel Motes, her main character, did, or willed, but in what he was unable to do. *Wise Blood* seemed then, and seems more so now, the supremely successful fictional treatment of the theme of original sin. "If I was in sin," Hazel said on one occasion, "I was in it before I ever committed any." Oddly, too, Miss O'Connor's intensely actual world reminds one incessantly of a more important, a more real invisible world. "Haze's shadow . . . was a thin nervous shadow walking backwards." The real persons, the substances, are the opposites of their own shadows. They are in darkness and their shadows testify to the light that is seeking them.

Flannery O'Connor's world is lonely, cruel, even perverse. In her stories the voice of a hidden narrator is almost always ironic. In "A Good Man is Hard to Find" the grandmother persists, in spite of her experience, in seeing the best in life. She cannot believe the murderer would shoot a lady. "I know you're a good man. You don't look a bit like you have common blood." For those who mistake the deep disturbance of humanity's common blood Miss O'Connor supplies the corrective pistol shot of "A Good Man is Hard to Find," or the crucial abandonment of the childish girl in "The Life You Save May Be Your Own," or the stolen wooden leg of "Good Country People," or the tractor plowing the broken back of the refugee in "The Displaced Person." No one experiencing Flannery O'Connor's world can doubt that, as Newman put it, "the human race is implicated in some terrible aboriginal calamity. It is out of joint with the purposes of its Creator."

Yet her world, especially in its violence, testifies to the importance of a heaven-seeking passion in the most unlikely characters. Sometimes, as in *The Violent Bear It Away*, Miss O'Connor formulates this view. Tarwater replies to Rayber's complicated talk about Baptism: "I ain't like you. All you can do is think what you would have done if you had done it. Not me. I can do it. I can act."

More often, Miss O'Connor presents her theme in metaphors, or in a rhythm of action reflected in the rhythms of her language. Hazel Motes' haunted imagination of death in life lives itself out in his memory of his dead mother, as he had seen her through a crack in her coffin. "He had seen the shadow that came down over her face and pulled her mouth down as if she wasn't any more satisfied dead than alive, as if she were going to spring up and shove the lid back and fly out and satisfy herself: but they shut it. He saw her in her sleep, terrible, like a huge bat, dart from the closing, fly out of there, but it was falling dark on top of her, closing down on her all the time."

Flannery O'Connor's realistic depiction of guilt, obsession and grotesque comedy was the work of her talent. The work of her genius was an angelic stirring of the waters of purgation. The visit of the angel was brief but it will not be forgotten.

Robert Drake
   Writer, Prof. University of Texas

The untimely death of Flannery O'Connor on August 3 at the age of 39 was not unexpected. For many years she had fought valiantly — and I think with some grim amusement — against poor health; and even at the onset of what proved to be her last illness she wrote, typically, that she "intended to survive this." That her determination was finally vain is sad but now irrelevant: she has passed into American literary history and left behind an impressive legacy of fiction — and that created in a productive period of less than 15 years. Her first novel, *Wise Blood*, appeared in 1952, followed by a collection of short stories, *A Good Man Is Hard to Find*, in 1955, and another novel, *The Violent Bear It Away*, in 1960. A final volume of stories is now being prepared by Farrar, Straus and Company for February publication.

She was often labeled "another Southern Gothic novelist" and once even "a Roman Catholic Erskine Caldwell," and her admirers and detractors were usually equally vociferous in praise or blame. But her unique achievement, I believe, was her depiction of the world in terms that were entirely those of the orthodox Christian. She made no apology for this point of view; she did not even try to make the conviction of sin and the good news "relevant" to moderns in the tortured, existentialist terms we have come to expect from some neo-Christian writers. There it was — the old, old story; and as far as Miss O'Connor was concerned you could take it or leave it. But in her world the same old imperative was still in force: somewhere along the line one had to choose this day whom he would serve. For her it was impossible to refuse to take sides. And her greatest villains were often Laodiceans of one sort or another, neither cold nor hot but craftily trying to beat the racket by the exercise of prudence, by calculation or scheming, by taking undue thought for the morrow — all practices often highly regarded in today's world.

Never perhaps was the question better posed in her work than by the Misfit, the pathological killer of the title story of *A Good Man Is Hard to Find*, which is perhaps her most typical story. Says the Misfit to the old grandmother, who has been reduced almost to idiocy by the terrifying experiences she has undergone: "Jesus was the only One that ever raised the dead, and He shouldn't have done it. He thrown everything off balance. If He did what He said, then it's nothing for you to do but throw away everything and follow Him, and if He didn't, then it's nothing for you to do but enjoy the few minutes you got left the best way you can - by killing somebody or burning down his house or doing some other meanness to him. No pleasure but meanness." Many of Miss O'Connor's villains, like "enlightened" people through the ages, are simply unwilling to make this choice. For good or ill, the Misfit *has* made a choice, as he indicates to the old lady when she begs him to pray to Jesus for help: "I don't want no help. I'm doing all right by myself." And this of course is also a familiar response to the gospel imperative — today as well as yesterday. And yet one feels that the Misfit has faced the issue squarely and made an honest choice, even if the wrong one. He has knowingly and willingly decided against Christ — not like the odious psychologist Rayber of *The Violent Bear It Away*, who prefers to view the whole business as just an outmoded superstition or a ghost that has to be laid.

The Great Displacer

Significantly, some of Miss O'Connor's women characters appear to be her greatest villains: she often seems to have believed in some sort of spiritual double standard. One character appearing again and again in her work is the widow or divorcee who considers herself to be as independent of God or the cosmic forces (those dark powers Hemingway referred to as "they") as she apparently is of sex. This woman usually lives with one or two children on a Georgia farm which she is determined to make pay off: the cows are going to give the required amount of milk, the Negro hands are *not* going to cheat her or get by with slacking, and every acre is going to produce. In short, the universe is going to come to heel. The gospel imperative to choose never affects this woman except as a source of embarrassment — a circumstance to which she has to give a kind of genteel lip service; but it is always lurking in the background ready to spring out — like "Christ the tiger" — to confront her with its grisly reality.

The central figure of the widow-divorcee is usually surrounded by spokesmen for the other side — sharecroppers or their wives or the farm Negroes — who, it often seems, take a kind of malevolent delight in opposing the woman's optimistic willfulness with perverse reminders of the intractability of both man and the universe, often in distorted gospel terms. In a sense they are like a Greek chorus, commenting on her folly and viewing its probable consequences with alarm. But the woman usually turns a deaf ear to such "nonsense" and proceeds sublimely down the road to destruction — and damnation. In "The Displaced Person," which may be Miss O'Connor's best story, the widow-divorcee, Mrs. McIntyre, has hired some Europeans displaced by events of World War II to work as hands on her farm: that will be one in the eye for those shiftless Negroes and poor whites who have probably been robbing her blind all these years. But, ironically, it is the displaced persons themselves who begin to displace not only the Negroes and poor whites but even Mrs. McIntyre and her whole way of life. And when she turns in anger on the Roman Catholic priest who made the initial arrangements for her and whose religion she really despises, he adjures her to remember her Christian duty and not turn the family away. Her reply is characteristic: "As far as I'm concerned, Christ was just another D.P." And she has spoken more wisely than she knows. Christ, as the New Testament teaches and as Miss O'Connor insists again and again, *is* a displaced person who is himself the great Displacer, perpetually an offense, an embarrassment and finally a scandal to the righteous, the genteel and the "enlightened": he *is* much too hairy for *them*. In a sense, he is the great Grotesque who, as Mrs. McIntyre charges, ostensibly of the D.P., has "upset the balance around here."

The Significance of the Grotesque

Critics have often commented on Miss O'Connor's predilection for the grotesque, and particularly on the fascination which physical deformity or imperfection seemed to hold for her. This is a familiar characteristic of contemporary southern writers — and not always a dramatically functional one either. But many critics have failed to see that her concern with the imperfect and the grotesque pointed to a conception of "straightness" and "oughtness" without which the imperfect and the grotesque are ultimately meaningless. (This can be contrasted with the effect achieved by some southern writers who simply pile up the horrors and hope for the best — or the worst. Erskine Caldwell and perhaps Tennessee Williams are cases in point.) Further, the very concept of the grotesque, which implies not only horror but a certain grim humor, seemed for her rooted in a realization not only of man's presumption but also of his sheer *folly* in trying to live on any terms but God's. Man is, finally, not only sinful but just plain silly in trying to "do all right by himself." She once explained southern writers' predilection for the grotesque — not without tongue in cheek, one suspects — by saying: "Well, maybe we're the only people left who can recognize a freak when we see it." But whatever role the grotesque plays in her fiction, it *is* always dramatically functional, never extraneous to the central design.

Miss O'Connor's prose style is often, one suspects, deliberately plain and graceless — almost at times ugly — a word for which she seemed to have a great deal of respect. In her stories it is always the genteel and the "enlightened," the do-gooders and the calculators, who hate "ugliness," whether it is manifested in physical deformity or the tangled skein of human existence or the scandalous message proclaimed by the Gospels — whatever contradicts the light, bright, deodorized and orderly universe of these deluded people. And one suspects that her prose is often ugly by intention — the inevitable embodiment of the harrowing evangel she proclaims, which is not peace but a sword.

Apocalyptic Perception

A staunch Roman Catholic born and bred in Georgia, she wrote mainly about southern fundamentalists or southern defectors from fundamentalist orthodoxy. There was nothing narrow or sectarian about her: she was catholic in the oldest and truest sense of the word. And like all good writers, she knew that her real subject was at her own doorstep, indeed was hardly to be found anywhere else. (She once wryly observed that if she should live in Japan 20 years and then try to write a story about the Japanese, the characters would all talk like Herman Talmadge.) And true to her heritage as a southerner, she had a healthy respect for *place*. (Of two well known American writers, the darlings of the New York literary scene, she once remarked, "You know what's the matter with them? They ain't *frum* anywhere.") But Georgia and evangelical Christianity were in her blood and bones for good or ill, and perhaps her greatest and most distinctive achievement lay in the fact that she remained faithful to what was best in both traditions while never turning a blind eye to what was ill. She was, like Faulkner or Hardy, a provincial who dealt in universals: her Georgia is the world, as are Yoknapatawpha and

Wessex.

Modest and soft-spoken, Miss O'Connor was nevertheless as direct and forthright in personal encounter as in her fiction — and not without traces of the same ironic humor. Her critical intelligence was of a very high order; and though her judgments of her contemporaries were sometimes harsh, they apparently were never motivated by envy or spite, and she was quick to give praise when she felt it was due. And though the vicissitudes of her own life might well have made her bitter, she did not seem to be so; nor for that matter did she appear to be "smiling through." She seemed rather to have turned on her own life the same searching glare she gave the world in her fiction, found what was good, what bad, and accepted it all as reality.

It is impossible at this moment to predict how Miss O'Connor's work will fare at the hands of literary historians or what her final place in literature will be. Yet we may hazard a few conjectures. For one thing, she *was* a minor writer and, I believe, a better short story writer than novelist. (Her novels are too skeletal, with not enough meat on the bones.) And she contributed nothing special to the form or technique of the short story: her principal distinction was in thematic treatment. Furthermore, the fact that she made no concessions to modern readers who did not share her view of man and the universe will inevitably deny her certain recognition. (Significantly, those same readers don't seem to have much trouble with Dante or Milton. After all, they're safely embalmed in the classical past — and their beatific and unsettling visions along with them. But as for a *modern* writer who really believes all that stuff, well really. . . .) But after all this has been said Miss O'Connor's work, though narrow in scope and limited in appeal, is unique; and it has an urgent intensity, even an ordered ferocity, that may ultimately give her a place in our fiction comparable in a minor way to that of Donne or Hopkins in English poetry. But to say more now would be presumptuous: we shall simply have to wait and see.

In her most recently published stories Miss O'Connor seemed to be taking a new turning. One senses a greater compassion for her damned, deluded characters, and once or twice she even allowed them to have a shattering insight into the error of their ways that did not destroy them in the very process — a Damascus Road experience perhaps, rather than a consuming vision of judgment. Whether this indicated a significant widening of her sympathies I cannot say: it certainly did not mean that she was growing more "tolerant." It may have represented a perception which had been there all along though temporarily submerged beneath her evangelistic portrayal of skewed man living in a bent world. And this final perception, I think, was not evangelistic but apocalyptic in that it did see ultimately behind the veil of darkness and deformity and terror and found there, at the last, light and order and peace.

(c) 1964 Christian Century Foundation. Reprinted by permission of the writer and the editor from "The Christian Century" magazine, Sept. 30, 1964.

P. Albert Duhamel
Critic, Writer, Prof. Boston College

The significance of Flannery O'Connor is to be found, at least in part, in her insistence upon the primacy of ideas. Writing at a time when the critical applause of the little magazines was soonest extended to the novelist who could display the greatest technical virtuosity in the use of the form, she was continually insistent that the continued viability of the form would depend upon its being used as a medium for the communication of impassioned commitment. Consequently she always remained a bit of a puzzle to the reviewers who were properly commendatory about her technical brilliance but who were not quite comfortable with the implications of the ideas in her stories. Some reviewers avoided the issue by qualifying her first novel as "arty fumbling" and Flannery O'Connor herself as "an interesting Southern stylist."

As the impressive achievement of her work continued to grow, she began to compel the critics to come to grips with what she was saying as well as how she was saying it. It seemed that she was little interested in any consideration of her work which did not give some consideration to content as well as form. Like Tarwater, the central character in her last published novel, *The Violent Bear It Away*, she insisted that people stand for something, that ideas were important, and that people had to get out of the excluded middle where it was fashionable to be for everything and consequently stand for nothing. So the critics who employed a rhetoric of non-commitment as far as her ideas were concerned badly misread her intentions and concerns.

The Wisdom of the Heart

Among the ideas which recur in her works and upon which she seemed to insist was an emphasis upon the wisdom of the heart and the dangers of an isolated reason which attempted to be a rule to itself. The same critics who were somewhat perplexed by her appeal for judgment in terms of content as well as technique were also prone to identify her closely with the Southern critics. She had little in common with Brooks, Warren, Ransom and Heilman but this devotion to a kind of humanism which looked upon the inheritance of northern Puritanism as producing a distorted, one-sided caricature of human nature. In an essay on "The Church and the Fiction Writer," she cited with great approval a remark of Monsignor Romano Guardini that the "roots of the eye are in the heart."

At times her fear of the essential inhumanity of any attitude which isolated reason from the total personality was most manifest in her suspicions of some aspects of modern science. In her story "The Life You Save May Be Your Own" she suggests that science knows less about essential human nature than the man of sympathy and common sense. For her the real knowledge was intuitive, emotional as well as intellectual, not clinical or aseptic. Thus in many of her stories, as in "The River," children are portrayed as possessed of an admirable vision. They see things as they are, wholly, directly, simply, as they are, and not as many adults who distort, rationalize and avoid what she called "an intimacy with creation."

This attempt to make people see things as they were was the recurring purpose of her works. Some readers found stories like "A Good Man Is Hard to Find" uninteresting because it seemed to lack detail or "Gothic" because it seemed to leave out so much of the ordinary to focus on the extraordinary. In all her stories Flannery O'Connor omitted the trivial to highlight the decisions and actions of moral significance. If her art was realistic, it was a realism in the philosophical sense of attempting a thorough catalogue of external detail.

In some ways she was concerned with focussing on the same aspects of essential reality as William Golding whose *Lord of the Flies* has provoked much recent discussion. Like Golding her characters are detailed enough to engage us as individuals but never so detailed as to distract from the essential type which they represent. Like Golding's novel and the medieval morality, the characters are there to evoke reflection, not to stir memory.

Her plots like her characters are uncluttered because this suited her purpose. She wanted to cram her novels with more matter and less art, to make men see creation properly, see their responsibilities, and to do something about them. In the climatic scene of *The Violent Bear It Away*, Tarwater, man tarred by sin but saved by the water of baptism, says to Rayber, the rationalist who is in touch with reality only through the help of science, "You can't just say 'No,' you got to 'Do' no. You got to show it. You got to show you mean it by doing it." Flannery O'Connor showed by her life as well as her work her impassioned commitment to ideas. No young writer who reflects on the state of the novel today, all sound but no fury, can afford to dedicate himself to his *metier* in the only way in which he can hope for significant success without pondering the significance of Flannery O'Connor.

Elizabeth Enright
Fiction Writer

Flannery O'Connor was a true original; we have many would-be's but few who really are. Besides a unique and icy wit, economy of style, and a marvelous ear, she could demonstrate a deep unsentimental tenderness, as in the story about the little boy and the river, the name of which escapes me now.

I would be less than honest if I said I liked everything she did. I did not. It seems to me that her preoccupation with mutilation, violence, and horror sometimes tended to pull her work out of shape, to force it dangerously towards the comic in a way not intended. But the fact remains that hers was a brilliant talent cut short far too soon.

James F. Farnham
at Western Reserve University in May, 1961, date of article.

One cannot skip to the lovely dawn of Easter morning without first having passed through Good Friday; the Resurrection itself is meaningless except as the culmination of the Passion. Those are the ever present themes that run through Flannery O'Connor's writing.

Had William Esty been thinking of this when he spoke of Miss O'Connor in the *Commonweal* (March 7, 1958), he might have found less validity in his reference to the "Paul Bowles-Flannery O'Connor cult of the Gratuitous Grotesque." Mr. Esty said of Miss O'Connor's grotesque characters and situations that "these over-ingenious horrifics are presumably meant to speak to us of the Essential Nature of Our Time, but when the very real and cruel grotesquerie of our world is converted into clever gimmicks for Partisan Review, we may be forgiven for reacting with the self-same disgust as the little old lady from Dubuque." Mr. Esty presumes rightly that Miss O'Connor is speaking to us of the Essential Nature of Our Time. Let us look at what the young lady from Milledgeville, Georgia, has said on the subject and then into her works.

Catholic Artist

First of all, Miss O'Connor is an artist, and Catholicism is one of her "circumstances," just as her living in the South is. This does not mean that her religion is a mere circumstantial accident, but it does mean that her religion is not the cause of, nor the cause for, the externalization of her vision as a Christian artist. The ultimate reason for her use of the grotesque is simply that this is the aspect of reality which her artistic talent is best able to produce. In a letter to the author she once said: "Essentially the reason my characters are grotesque is because it is the nature of my talent to make them so. To some extent, the writer can choose his subject; but he can never choose what he is able to make live. It is characters like The Misfit and the Bible Salesman that I can make live."

Miss O'Connor writes, then, of the ugly simply because she can give life to the ugly. This is the ultimate explanation, for we are not called upon to concern ourselves with the ways and means by which talents are allotted.

Of course, given this talent for the grotesque, there is the question of what Miss O'Connor is to do with it, what meaning she gets out of it or puts into it. She does not like the sentimentalism of much contemporary Christian art; and, while never allowing her artistic talents merely to be turned to antisentimentalistic propaganda, she attempts to combat sentimentalism, her chief tool being the use of the grotesque. She sees modern man as an often grotesque figure, a caricature of his true self, and in showing what man is she is showing what he could be. It seems to be Miss O'Connor's intention never to let us think of man's salvation unless we are aware — painfully at times — of what the Passion was intended to redeem.

Redemption Theme

The central theme found in Flannery O'Connor's writing is the redemption of man; but, since her talent inclines her toward the portrayal of sin, she shows the effects of the redemption (i.e., grace) in a negative manner. She reflects the beauty of virtue by showing the ugliness of its absence. In her essay on "The Fiction Writer and His Country" she writes:

"My own feeling is that writers who see by the light of their Christian faith will have, in these times, the sharpest eyes for the grotesque, for the perverse and for the unacceptable.... Redemption is meaningless unless there is cause for it in the actual life we live.

If Miss O'Connor could believe that her audience is one which thinks within the basic Christian rationale, she would find it unnecessary to dwell upon the deformation of humanity. But, since she writes for an audience which she thinks is to a great extent blind to grace, she feels that she must show them how bad they are, not simply how good somebody else is. When you cannot assume, she says in "The Fiction Writer and His Country," that your audience is aware of grace, "you have to make your vision apparent by shock — to the hard of hearing you shout, and for the almost blind you draw large and startling figures." Flannery O'Connor does not shout of the ugliness of man deformed by sin because of any gratuitous pleasure involved in her writing process. Rather, she is a Christian writer acutely aware of grace, a writer whose talents impel her to the portrayal of a contemporary society deformed by its disavowal of grace.

Disavowal of Grace

This is her esthetic of the physically and spiritually ugly. She sees society very much aware of its abnegation of grace; indeed, it is their realization of loss which makes her characters so awful. They are not dumb creatures plodding ahead in stolid unknowing. For the most part, they are aware that there is some great void in their existences. The Misfit, for example, in "A Good Man Is Hard To Find," as he prepares to murder a family just starting on its vacation, says to the grandmother:

"Jesus thrown everything off balance. It was the same with Him as with me, except He hadn't committed any crime and they could prove I had committed one because they had the papers on me. He thrown everything off balance. If He did what He said, then it's nothing for you to do but throw away everything and follow Him, and if He didn't then it's nothing for you to do but enjoy the few minutes you got left the best way you can — by killing somebody or burning down his house or doing some other meanness to him. No pleasure but meanness."

> "I am no disbeliever in spiritual purpose and no vague believer."

Certainly, Christ's Passion has influenced this man, but he has perverted the grace. Here is humanity in its suffering, but the suffering is without meaning. "I call myself The Misfit . . . because I can't make what all I done wrong fit what all I gone through in punishment." The redemption of man is perverted, and without grace man finds suffering and injustice maddeningly incomprehensible. Miss O'Connor's most evil characters are acutely aware of Christ, making their pain more intense by their blasphemy of Him.

Thus it is with the Bible salesman in "Good Country People." While all along the cynical young woman named Hulga (her real name was "Joy" but she relished the cacophony of "Hulga") thought that she was leading the Bible salesman to his seduction in the barn, he was in fact intent upon stealing her artificial leg. After he has revealed to her that his suitcase contains not only Bibles which he sells, but dirty playing cards, contraceptives and whiskey as well, her complacent cynicism collapses. "Aren't you just good country people?" she murmurs. "Yeah," he sneers, "but it ain't held me back none." "You're a perfect Christian," she hisses. To which he replies in, a lofty and indignant tone, "I hope you don't think . . . I believe in that crap — I been believing in nothing ever since I was born ! "

Perversion of Grace

Here, again, Miss O'Connor does people who have never been touched by grace. They are painfully aware of grace, but their lives are focused upon its perversion. The salesman under the guise of spreading the Word of God is actually disbursing evil.

Tom T. Shiftlet in "The Life You Save May be Your Own" is constantly appalled by the evil men do. "Nothing is like it used to be," he says. "The world is almost rotten." After marrying the idiot daughter of the farm woman for whom he works so that he can get her old Ford, he leaves his bride asleep in a roadside restaurant. Later, a young hitchhiker, in response to Shiftlet's sentimental reference to his sweet old mother, replies that "My old woman is a flea bag and yours is a stinking polecat." Shiftlet is horrified by the evil within the human heart and he races into Mobile full of righteous anger, invoking God to "Break forth and wash the slime from the earth." This character, like most in Miss O'Connor's grotesque gallery of humanity, has "a moral intelligence," so he says, but so perverted is it that grace has given way to evil. Miss O'Connor's characters are not gratuitously grotesque; they are grotesque because she sees reality without grace grotesque.

If such as The Misfit, the Bible salesman and Tom T. Shiftlet are images of graceless humanity, Hazel Motes in Miss O'Connor's first novel, *Wise Blood*, is an almost metaphysical perversion of the Savior. Haze envisions himself as a new redeemer:

"I preach the Church Without Christ. I'm member and preacher to that church where the blind don't see and the lame don't walk and what's dead stays that way. Ask me about that church and I'll tell you it's the church that the blood of Jesus don't foul with redemption ....

I'm going to preach it to whoever'll listen at whatever place. I'm going to preach there was no fall because there was nothing to fall from, and no redemption because there was no fall, and no judgement because there wasn't the first two. Nothing matters but that Jesus was a liar."

Haze cannot ignore redemption and cannot escape it. His only salvation lies in a new dispensation of the utter perversion of grace. His grandfather used to tell him that "he had been redeemed and Jesus wasn't going to leave him ever. Jesus would never let him forget he was redeemed." Haze had never sought redemption, but redemption had always hounded him. Throughout his life he has been abnormally aware of original sin. As a boy, he had put small stones in his shoes, laced them up very tightly, and walked through the woods to expiate for his sense of inherited guilt. Near the end of his public life after he had blinded himself with lime to confess his nihilistic religion of the denial of Christ and of grace, his landlady discovered in his shoes gravel, broken glass and pieces of small stone. In explanation he merely answered: "To pay."

Tragic Figure

Out of context these descriptions of Hazel Motes might seem morbid; but in context they present a figure of almost heroically tragic proportions, a figure reminiscent of Milton's Satan, a Christ of Evil. Consumed by evil as he is, Haze like Satan cannot ignore nor even long be away from Christ. His suffering is the realization of loss, of man's fall. So darkened is his spirit by the chaos of his soul that grace cannot penetrate it, and he plunges deeper into darkness. This, then, is Flannery O'Connor's theme, the fall of man brought up to date.

As Hazel Motes is a graceless Christ, so Francis Marion

Tarwater of her recent novel, *The Violent Bear It Away*, is a perverted prophet of Old Testament stature. "The boy was very proud that he had been born in a wreck. He had always felt that it set him apart... that the plan of God for him was special." His face "expressed the depth of human perversity, the deadly sin of rejecting defiantly one's obvious good." His first mission was to baptize his cousin, and this he did by drowning the idiot child. We leave him at the end of the book with his public career as prophet before him. "His singed eyes... seemed already to envision the fate that awaited him but he moved steadily on, his face set toward the dark city, where the children of God lay sleeping."

> *"I see from the standpoint of Christian orthodoxy."*

It is ironic that in one of the very few instances ("The River") where one can see grace to be in any way efficacious, it is in a child: in Harry Ashfield who renamed himself "Bevel" after the country preacher who baptized him at a revival meeting. The preacher had said: "You'll be washed in the river of suffering, son, and you'll go by the deep river of life." Bevel accepted the words literally and arose one morning, before his hung-over parents were up, and left home to re-enter the river. He found it difficult at first to enter under the water, but the waiting current caught him like a long gentle hand and pulled him swiftly forward and down. For an instant he was overcome with surprise; then since he was moving quickly and he knew that he was getting somewhere, all his fury and his fear left him.

Miss O'Connor allows this child, who took the words of redemption literally, to find salvation. Such characters as Hazel Motes, the Bible salesman, The Misfit, Tom T. Shiftlet and Marion Tarwater are so warped by their disavowal of grace that she cannot conceive of their being saved. Only in the ironically and pathetically contradictory sense of a redemption in evil can they be said to find self-realization or salvation.

In "The Fiction Writer and His Country," Miss O'Connor quotes Cyril of Jerusalem to his catechumens: "The dragon sits by the side of the road, watching those who pass. Beware lest he devour you." She comments that "It is of this mysterious passage past him, or into his jaws, that stories of any depth will always be concerned to tell." Much of the world's literature is concerned with man's relation to sin and evil. This is Flannery O'Connor's concern.

Her particular talent is externalized by giving life to the grotesquerie of evil, but hers is not the "cult of the Gratuitous Grotesque." One word can make a great difference. Grotesque she is, but certainly not gratuitously grotesque.

Reprinted by permission of AMERICA, National Catholic Weekly Review, N.Y. (c) 1961

Sr. Mariella Gable, O. S. B.
Writer, Prof. College of St. Benedict, Minn.

Flannery O'Connor was the most gifted American writer of the mid-century, endowed with a cluster of dazzling talents which added up to pure genius. A brilliant stylist, she was immediately recognized by the literary *haut monde*, though she was carelessly lumped with other outstanding Southern writers as another purveyor of the gratuitously grotesque. Nothing could have been less true. She somewhere, somehow early in life discovered the magnetic power of truth — that which lies at the vortex of reality and explains the dizzying whirlpool. She saw that the whole meaning of life centered in the Incarnation. She said:

> I see from the standpoint of Christian orthodoxy. This means that for me the meaning of life is centered in our Redemption by Christ and that what I see in the world I see in relation to that. I don't think that this is a position which can be taken half way or one that is particularly easy in these times to make transparent in fiction. (Flannery O'Connor, "The Fiction Writer and His Country," in Granville Hicks, ed., *The Living Novel*, p. 162.)

Difficult as it was to make such a viewpoint clear in fiction she did accomplish this miracle over and over again. Particularly in "The Displaced Person" where she makes is transparently clear that all who do not believe in the redemption are displaced persons. Their native country is Christianity. Robert Fitzgerald points out that her stories "not only imply, they as good as state again and again that estrangement from Christian plenitude is estrangement from the true country of man." (*Sewanee Review*, LXX, p. 394.)

But more than being a committed Christian she was the first great writer of ecumenical fiction anywhere in the world. Though she was only a month away from death, she exerted herself to tell me that my article, "The Ecumenic Core in the Fiction of Flannery O'Connor" (*American Benedictine Review*, June 1964, pp. 127-143) came nearer the truth about her writing than any other criticism. With characteristic humility she said, "I shall learn from it myself and save my breath by referring other people to it." Her people in and around Georgia and Tennessee were the people of the Bible Belt who lived with Scripture. They were marinated in the word of God. She saw with Ignatius Hunt, O.S.B., that Scripture is the stepping stone to ecumenism. How true was an observation she made in a letter to me:

> I am more and more impressed with the amount of Catholicism that fundamentalist Protestants have been able to retain. Theologically our differences with them are on the nature of the Church, not on the nature of God or our obligations to Him. (Letter to Sister Mariella Gable, May 4, 1963.)

Because she saw this truth with great clarity, felt it in the core of her being, she chose her characters from the Bible Belt (very infrequently included a Catholic) yet elicited from her fiction some of the profoundest Catholic truths ever concretized in fiction. She wrote for an unbelieving world, not for Catholics. Her fiction was Christian in a new and startling way which shocked and pained many readers.

Like Christ who found the poor suitable for His friendship, she remarked of the characters in her stories:

> When I look at the stories I have written I find they are for the most part about people who are poor, who are afflicted in both mind and body, who have little —

or at best a distorted - sense of spiritual purpose, and
whose actions apparently do not give the reader a
great assurance of the joy of life. (Flannery O'Connor,
"The Fiction Writer and His Country," Granville
Hicks, ed., *The Living Novel*. p. 161.)

People complained about the grotesquerie and ugliness of her stories.
Why did she not paint Christianity so that it looked desirable? In a
letter to me she answered this key question with such wisdom that I
believe a large part of it should be shared at this time with the public
so shocked at her death, still so bewildered by much of her fiction.
She who realized that the Incarnation had transformed the whole
status of man took an incarnational view of fiction so profound in its
implications for the artist that it might, if it were suitably
apprehended by many, transform the whole aspect of what has been
so objectionably called "Catholic fiction."

Milledgeville, Georgia 4 May 1963

Dear Sister Mariella,

. . .

When they ask you to make Christianity
desirable they are asking you to describe its essence,
not what you see. Ideal Christianity doesn't exist,
because anything the human being touches, even
Christian truth he deforms slightly in his own image.
Even the saints do this. I take it to be the effects of
Original Sin and I notice that Catholics often act as if
that doctrine is always perverted and always an
indication of Calvinism. They read a little corruption
as total corruption. The writer has to make the
corruption believable before he can make the grace
meaningful.

The tendency of people who ask questions like
this is always toward the abstract and therefore
toward allegory, thinness, and ultimately what they
are looking for is an apologetic fiction. The best of
them think: Make it look desirable because it is

desirable. And the rest of them think: Make it look desirable so I won't look like a fool for holding it. In a really Christian culture of real believers this wouldn't come up.

I know that the writer does call up the general and maybe the essential through the particular, but this general and essential is still deeply embedded in mystery. It is not answerable to any of our formulas. It doesn't rest finally in a statable kind of solution. It ought to throw you back on the living God. Our Catholic mentality is great on paraphrase, logic, formula instant and correct answers. We judge before we experience and never trust our faith to be subjected to reality, because it is not strong enough. And maybe in this we are wise. I think this spirit is changing on account of the council but the changes will take a long time to soak through.

And the fanatics. People make a judgment of fanaticism by what they are themselves. To a lot of Protestants I know, monks and nuns are fanatics, none greater. And to a lot of monks and nuns I know, my Protestant prophets are fanatics. For my part, I think the only difference between them is that if you are a Catholic and have this intensity of belief you join the convent and are heard no more; whereas if you are a Protestant and have it, there is no convent for you to join and you go about the world getting into all sorts of trouble and drawing the wrath of people who don't believe anything much at all down on your head.

This is one reason why I can write about Protestant believers better than Catholic believers — because they express their belief in diverse kinds of dramatic action which is obvious enough for me to catch. I can't write about anything subtle. Another thing, the prophet is a man apart. He is not typical of a group. Old Tarwater is not typical of the Southern Baptist, of the Southern Methodist. Essentially he's a crypto-Catholic. When you leave a man alone with his Bible and the Holy Ghost inspires him, he's going to be a Catholic one way or another, even though he knows nothing about the visible Church. His kind of Christianity may not be socially desirable, but it will be real in the sight of God. If I set myself to write about a socially desirable Christianity, all the life would go out of what I do. And if I set myself to write about the essence of Christianity, I would have to quit writing fiction or either become another person.

...

I probably have enough stories for a collection but I want to wait and see what this turns out to be that I am writing on now. Then perhaps if it turns out to be a long story, I'll put them all together in a collection.

...

As everyone knows by now, she had completed plans before she died for a collection of her stories to be published in February 1965 under the magnificent title, *All That Rises Must Converge*, a quotation from her favorite philosopher, Teilhard de Chardin.

Fourteen months before she died she wrote me the following eloquent comment on the point she had reached as a writer. She had already begun a new novel, *Why Do the Heathen Rage ?* But she felt that she had reached a milestone and that her first great contribution had been completed. Here are her own words:

I've been writing eighteen years and I've reached the point where I can't do again what I know I can do well, and the larger things that I need to do now, I doubt my capacity for doing.

Perhaps her doubt indicated that it was not God's will for her to continue to write. About the excellence of her ecumenical fiction she entertained not the slightest doubt. I can still hear her say with the assurance that she had touched eternal truth in *The Violent Bear It Away*: "I can wait fifty years, a hundred years for it to be understood." She noted how readers, even Catholic readers who should have known better, identified with Rayber, the materialist, rather than with the fanatic, Old Tarwater. "It will take a while," she smiled, "for people to see what I mean." Her confidence in her ability to communicate the most important truth in the world was part of her humility.

To talk with her was one of the most unforgettable experiences of a lifetime. Simple, unpretentious, humble, gay with a sense of humor which saw our absurdities as matter for laughter, her direct honesty even made persons who thought they habitually spoke the truth look like liars. I have never known one so habitually at home with truth. God gave her a magnificent work to do. That He took her from us is proof positive that she had completed that work. It remains now for us to understand it truly.

Harold Gardiner, S. J.
Writer, Critic, Lit. Ed., AMERICA

Though others who are contributing to this appreciation of Flannery O'Connor will almost certainly speak of her as a Christian and Catholic artist, I must beg leave to address these very few remarks to that same point. Perhaps it will be found that I approach this aspect of her in a slightly different way, for I wish to deal with her not as a creative artist, but as a critic. I must frankly admit that I have not read all of her critical work, mainly because it is scattered over a number of journals. I do remember, however, and with great admiration, the article she wrote for *America* (March 30, 1957), in which she "justified" her Catholic approach to creative writing; far from being cabined by her faith and confined by it, she states, she found that it gave to her vision added dimensions and depths of realization.

The casual reader most likely misses this dimension in Miss O'Connor's work because she did not intrude her grasp of the faith in any overt fashion; she did not overtly strike the stance of a Catholic writer either in her creative work or in her criticism. I believe she would have fully concurred with this passage from *Poetry and Morality* by Vincent Buckley:

Christianity should not be used merely as an objective

"standard" not because it is too small, but because it is too huge. The attempt to "complete" literary criticism "by criticism from a definite ethical and theological standpoint" [the phrase is Eliot's] arises from the desire to have an artist who will offer us an account of life which is totally Christian: and that is impossible. No creative artist exhausts art or Christianity. . . . The life of Christianity is the life of the Church, and this is infinitely greater and more embracing than the whole tradition of literature. All that an artist can offer is his personal response to the growth of his personal wisdom. . . .

Mr. Buckley is overtly speaking of literary criticism, and Miss O'Connor's criticism manifests this quality. From all we know of her personal life (and from clear manifestations of it in such a work as *Mary Anne*), it is evident that she grew all through her short life in a "personal response to the growth of personal wisdom," and this is manifest in her critical attitudes as well as in her creative work.

I think that a touchstone to an appreciation of O'Connor is to be found in this further observation of Buckley: "Christianity is more relevant to literary criticism the more inward and unobtrusive it is." The same can be said of the creative work of the Catholic writer, and the brief corpus of Miss O'Connor's work is a monument to the true inwardness of her realization of the liberating wisdom of the faith.

We may with all justification lament the passing of such a superb (though still developing) creative talent; we should mourn as well the void in Catholic literary criticism that her death has left.

Caroline Gordon
Novelist, Critic, Teacher

Flannery O'Connor is dead at the age of thirty-nine and already paeans of praise are being raised in her honor. Some of the praise is based on the fact that her books have been widely distributed and is so undiscriminating as hardly to honor this serious and accomplished fiction writer. Perhaps an attempt to appraise her peculiar and novel achievement is the greatest tribute her admirers can pay her. It seems to me that her chief distinction lies in the fact that almost alone among her contemporaries, she succeeded in wedding a revolutionary technique to its appropriate subject matter.

This technique has been accessible to every maker of fiction since the year 1 *Anno Domini* and was widely used until the beginnings of the Renaissance. Since that time fewer and fewer writers have used it and in our own day it has become almost obsolete — or, at least, so hedged about with superstitions and taboos that the writer who used it ran the risk not only of having next to no readers but of having his work persistently misrepresented. Miss O'Connor's stories, however, are all about the operations of supernatural grace in the lives of natural men and women. Such operations are infinitely various but so delicate that they have eluded some of the subtlest writers. In her last (as yet unpublished) short story, "Parker's Back," Miss O'Connor seems to have succeeded where the great Flaubert failed: in the dramatization of that particular heresy which denies Our Lord corporeal substance. We do not naturally like anything which is unfamiliar. No wonder Miss O'Connor's writings have baffled the reviewers — so much so that they have reached for any cliché they could lay hold of in order to have some way of apprehending this original and disturbing work.

Nancy Hale
Fiction Writer, Critic

Flannery O'Connor's death, tragically early in time, cuts off short a growing part of American writing as well. That we will not be having any more of her work does not simply mean we will not be having any more like what she had already written. Each thing she wrote was a development from what had been before, a pushing out into unexplored literary territory. Not least of her conquests among these wilds, it seems to me, was her solving of the problem of how a woman writer is to write about the most brutal and carnal facts of life without causing the reader embarrassment. The reader of Flannery O'Connor never knew what was happening to him, or rather, how it happened — she was that much in control of the situation. She was a pathfinder in the use of her material, a mistress of form; wise in what Faulkner called the frail and fragile heart of humanity.

Elizabeth Hardwick
  Writer, Critic, Novelist

  Flannery O'Connor was a brilliant writer. Her fiction was, above all, unexpected and disturbing and she herself was an unexpected, extraordinary person, not much like other people. The cruel suffering she endured for such a long time, her death at the age of thirty-eight, fill those who knew her with pain. I first met her when she was very young and writing *Wise Blood*. I remember that I found that book somewhat difficult to like at the beginning. It was so fierce, so hard, so plainly, down-rightly unusual. And yet, of course, I did finally like *Wise Blood* (you can't easily hold out against Hazel Motes) even if I did like better the marvelous short stories, collected in *A Good Man is Hard to Find*. But where had all this come from? one was always asking oneself. The author had led a secluded life. She was a Roman Catholic, of Irish extraction, born and brought up in Georgia. Most of all she was like some quiet, puritanical convent girl from the harsh provinces of Canada. Her work was utterly different; it was Southern, rural, wicked, with a nearly inexplicable knowledge of the deformed and sinful, the all-too-deeply experienced. She was fascinated by street preachers, ignorant and insisting fundamentalists, by maimed persons with a matchless commitment to their grotesque destinies. She saw everything with a severe humor, local enough in accent, but more detached, more difficult to define than most other Southern writing. You'll have to call *A Good Man is Hard to Find* a "funny" story even though six people are killed in it.
  Good Country People is an astonishing work which Allen Tate has called "the most powerful story of maimed souls by a contemporary writer." The story starts off with an overblown, exaggerated cast: a foolish mother, her daughter, Joy, who has a wooden leg and a degree in philosophy, a verbose Bible salesman. These characters are, in outline, fit only for a dirty joke, and the plot continues accordingly. The Bible salesman seduces the girl with the wooden leg in a hay loft. His Bible is a fake one. When he opens it up, instead of the Scriptures out comes a whiskey flask, a pack of dirty postcards, and a box of condoms. The salesman is wildly

aroused by the wooden leg and makes off with it, leaving Joy stranded in the hay loft. But the story is a superb success. It is wise and memorable and entirely believable. The girl, Joy, has that sullen anxiety, along with a natural superiority, that make the assertion of her intellectuality and the philosophy degree convincing. She is an atheist, trying to hold on to her good sense, against her platitudinous mother. Her humiliation by the Bible salesman is again one of those meanly humorous and yet scorching scenes that are characteristic of Flannery O'Connor's fiction.

No doubt every sort of religious or moral stress might be put upon this story; indeed it seems to demand it. In everything of Flannery O'Connor's we are aware of her intense preoccupation with the ragged remnants of Protestantism, those hungry sectarians, those wandering souls with the Answer, those diviners of Revelations, and receivers of code messages from the Holy Spirit. Nearly every plot development turns in this direction. In *Wise Blood*, Hazel Motes set up his own religion: The Church without Christ. "I'm member and preacher to that church where the blind don't see and the lame don't walk and what's dead stays that way."

Her second novel, *The Violent Bear it Away*, is about Baptism, the duty to which these mad St. Johns of the Southern wilderness are called. This novel ends in an unbearable immolation scene and is one of the strangest productions in recent American fiction. It is grotesque, painful, again "funny," and entirely original in spirit and theme. Flannery O'Connor's backwoodsmen need God and Faith, and especially revelation; but every mad one of them is on his own. Perhaps it is this concentration on the violent and crippling aloneness of these zealots that might be called "Catholic." By this I mean that a Roman Catholic working out his salvation through the observances of the church is peculiarly sensitive to the incoherence of these lonely priests, each making his own religion and his own canon law. And yet I cannot help but want to hold out against a too eager "Catholic" appropriation of these stories. It has sometimes seemed to me that the author had something in her too of the girl with the wooden leg who suffered defeat at the hands of fools and frauds and wondered about good country people and good "Chrustians," as her people pronounce it, alike.

Flannery O'Connor's brilliant talent was of that sort that has a contradiction in every pore. She was indeed, a Catholic writer, also a Southern writer; but neither of these traditions prepares us for the oddity and beauty of her lonely fiction.

John Hawkes
> Novelist

If we think of Flannery O'Connor as a brilliant but highly disturbing visionary writer, someone whose magical black humor and ruthless fictional stance kept her quite outside the circle of ordinary human response — so that she attacked earthly pretension relentlessly and treated even her most serious religious themes and materials comically — it then seems all the more important, for me at least, to remember that the word with which she invariably ended her letters was "Cheers." This word, I think, represents the attitude she took toward life. It perhaps best conveys the economy, energy, pleasure and grace out of which she constructed her amazingly detached and often marvelously distorted fictions. And it is an indication of the tone she adopted toward death and toward her own suffering. But if Flannery O'Connor was apparently invulnerable or even indifferent to mortality, she nonetheless gave the impression of living every moment of her life with a special quickness. So now it seems important to stress the sprightly warmth and wry, engaging, uninhibited humanity of a writer commonly described as one of America's coldest and most shocking comic writers.

Behind her thoroughly original, uncompromising, hard-minded view of the world lay a kind of crouching innocence; her extraordinary and sometimes brutal strength as a writer was based on a unique purity and gentleness of spirit. She leaves us the beauty of the paradox, which is a great gift.

Granville Hicks
> Critic, Writer, Editor

Flannery O'Connor was one of the most richly gifted fiction

writers of our time. She often said that her particular view of life was a result of her being a Catholic and a Southerner, and both religion and regionalism are important in the understanding of her work. But her quality as a writer cannot be defined in terms of any two or two hundred influences. She saw what she saw, and somehow she discovered or developed exactly the right way to articulate and communicate her vision. In spite of her infirmities, she was constantly acquiring greater and greater mastery of her materials. Although her body of work was comparatively small, it will not be forgotten for a long time.

Frank L. Hoskins, Jr.
Editor, *"Studies in Short Fiction"*

It was lunch time on a bright, hot day in early September when we drove into the county town of Baldwin County, in a neighboring state. We found an air-conditioned lunchroom, sat down at the counter, and ordered a ham on rye, no mayonnaise. The waitress, fiftyish, dumpy, and ample-bosomed, asked, "Will it be anything to drink?" We ordered a large RC; and while we waited for our sandwich, we noticed that the waitress, whose skill in serving her customers yielded only to her volubility, had an unhappy set to her mouth. We ventured to hope that the world was treating her right. "Thangs hasn't been right since my old man was murdered." This being considerably more than we had reckoned on, we sought, for several seconds, a suitable response.
"Someone shoot him?"
"No. He was cut up with a knife."
"How perfectly horrible!" we said. "What'd they do to the man who did it?"
"They ain't never found out who done it."
We were speechless.
"I think I know who done it. But it ain't no evidence."
We looked quizzical.
"Four of 'em done it. They cut him up and threw him on the highway. He was cut up so bad we c'tn't bury him in his clothes nohow."
Having somehow choked down our sandwich, we ordered

black coffee and maneuvered the conversation to more general considerations. The cashier, a lantern-jawed, grey-haired woman wearing bifocals framed by tortoise shell, joined the discussion when we recalled, *a propos* of man's hatefulness, that we had recently read in the papers about a woman's drowning in the presence of several onlookers not one of whom bestirred himself to rescue her. "And what about them folks up nawth," she said, "who watched a woman bein' stabbed to death and didn't do nuthin'? It's a heap of wickedness in this here world."

We had to agree.

We asked the waitress, who, we learned, was a native of east Tennessee, whether she thought people hereabouts were more sinful than people at home. "It's sin everwhirr. They ain't no worse here than other places I bin. But it's some god-awful mean ones here."

This was Flannery O'Connor country all right. In fact, we were in Milledgeville, Georgia, where, we discovered not really to our surprise, that O'Connor characters actually live and breathe.

After paying our bill we left the lunchroom and walked down Hancock Street to the Mary Vinson Memorial Library, where Mrs. Royce Smith, the Librarian, and her assistants had set up a display of O'Connorana. We asked Mrs. Smith what Flannery O'Connor read and learned that she seldom used the public library because of her large library at "Andalusia," the O'Connor place outside Milledgeville, on the highway to Atlanta.

We also visited Memory Hill Cemetery, out Liberty Street from Hancock, where we paid our respects to the mortal remains of Flannery O'Connor. Her body lies in a family plot, and, in early September, the red soil on the grave had not yet settled down to surface level. Also the grave lacked, at that time, a stone.

At mid-afternoon, under the bluest of blue skies, we left Milledgeville, crossed the Oconee River, and drove through a pacific of piney woods back to South Carolina. Our thoughts all the way home returned frequently to Flannery O'Connor's dry, detached sardonic rendering of the human condition. Between the lines of her fiction we never fail, though, to sense a deep compassion devoid of sentimentality. We thought of her unerring eye and ear; of her extraordinary talent for evoking verbally the deep South, where oversimplified religious beliefs of the "White," semi-literate fundamentalists could, however, incongruously, be a path to salvation; the kudzu, which threatens to bury a culture; the ubiquitous mockingbirds, redbirds, and used car lots; the impertinent highways through the endless pine forests; the collard greens cooked with salt pork; the red dirt; the shell houses and the chihuahuas; and the squirrel tails on car radio antennas. We thought, too, of the stories and the novels that Flannery O'Connor would have written had she not been ill; had she lived a normal span of years. We thought of suffering and of the Devil among us and of human indomitableness and of the mystery of art and of Divine Providence.

Miserere nobis.

Sr. M. Joselyn, O. S. B.
Prof. College of St. Scholastica, Minn.

I may as well admit — however frivolous it sounds amidst our sorrow at her passing — that Flannery O'Connor will always be associated in my mind with . . . peacocks! Not just because I revere her use of that bird in a fine short story, "The Displaced Person;" not only because of the pure charm of her *Holiday* piece, "Living with a Peacock" with its gorgeous photo of the cock by Carroll Seghers; not merely because some of Miss O'Connor's letters to me told about peacocks and one included a portion of a feather with a great golden "sun" in it. I would not say either that the peacock is in any way a *symbol* of Flannery O'Connor, or she of it. But the association is there.

Perhaps it is because the peacocks freed so much for our delight that was in Flannery O'Connor, helped her so greatly to show us what she was, became her "objective correlative," if one wants to be literary about it. You will know what I mean — here is an anecdote she tells about one of her birds:

> An old man and five or six white-haired children were piling out the back of the automobile as the bird approached. Catching sight of him, the children stopped in their tracks and stared, plainly hacked to find this superior figure blocking their path. There was silence as the bird regarded them, his head drawn back at its most majestic angle, his folded train

glittering behind him in the sunlight.

"Whut is thet thang?" one of the small boys asked finally in a sullen voice.

The old man got out of the car and was gazing at the peacock with an astounded look of recognition. "I ain't seen one of them since my grand-daddy's day," he said, respectfully removing his hat. "Folks used to have 'em, but they don't no more."

"Whut is it?" the child asked again in the same tone he had used before.

"Churren," the old man said, "that's the king of the birds!"

The children received this information in silence. After a minute they climbed back into the car and continued from there to stare at the peacock, their expressions annoyed, as if they disliked catching the old man in the truth.

There is a marvelous, deep-rooted congruity between this story and her saying, "when fiction is made according to its nature, it should reinforce our sense of the supernatural by grounding it in concrete observable reality" and

> It is generally supposed, and not least by Catholics, that the Catholic who writes fiction is out to use fiction to prove the truth of his faith or, at the least, to prove the existence of the supernatural. He may be.

Or take this observation on the peacock: "The cock's plumage requires two years to attain its pattern, and for the rest of his life this chicken will act as though he designed it himself" and see how it dovetails into "I'm interested in the old Adam. He just talks southern because I do." Or again,

> Frequently the cock combines the lifting of his tail with the raising of his voice. He appears to receive through his feet some shock from the center of the earth, which travels upward through him and is

released: *Ee-oo-ii! Eee-ooo-ii!* To the melancholy this sound is melancholy and to the hysterical it is hysterical. To me it has always sounded like a cheer for an invisible parade.

Precisely the same quality of honesty, of realism, lies in her other remark, "I take it a good story would be one which continues to rattle on at a great rate at the same time that it reaches a profound level of meaning. . . . I'm a very traditional sort of writer and I'm content to try to tell a good story as I've just defined it." And: "The Lord can use anything, but you just think He shouldn't have to."

Flannery O'Connor wrote, "The peacock likes to sit on gates or fence posts and allow his tail to hang down. A peacock on a fence post is a superb sight. Six or seven peacocks on a gate are beyond description. . . ." The most subtle trail of my associations leads to the peacock's ancient identity with the heavenly and eternal — how natural for its sublime beauty to lead that way! — and with Christ's divinity. It seems to me that Flannery O'Connor must know these things by vision now, and not merely through the earthly way of watching and listening, and I should not be surprised if she is now more rapt than ever before with the bird of the resurrection.

> ". . . for me the meaning of life is centered in our Redemption by Christ and what I see in the world I see in its relation to that. I don't think that this is a position that can be taken half-way or one that is particularly easy in these times to make transparent in fiction."

Frank Kermode
Critic, Writer, Prof. U. of Manchester, England

Flannery O'Connor is not yet widely read in England. I read *The Violent Bear It Away* while on a visit to the U.S.A. in 1961, at the instance of Allen Tate. It was at once evident that the author had a powerful and interesting vision, and I understood the special regard in which she was held by some of the young literary people I encountered. At the time of her death I was teaching a small graduate seminar at Rutgers. We were discussing *Lear*; at some point in the debate a student brought up, with a strange bit inevitable propriety, the fact of Miss O'Connor's death, which the *Times* had that morning announced. The effect of this on those who had not heard the news was both appropriate and impressive; it was a kind of deep dismay, as experienced by men and women devoted to literature and at that very moment deeply involved in the greatest of all tragedies; one felt for a second that complex union of reality and justice which tragedy affords, but this time one felt it in life. And this was also appropriate, since we were silent for one who had known how to enact that very union.

Francis L. Kunkel
 Writer, Prof. St. John's U., N. Y.

Often overlooked is the varied humor throughout Flannery O'Connor's work. Even her short stories display comic breadth. "The Artificial Nigger," for example, ranges from the ludicrous and howlingly funny to the grim and quietly ironic. Miss O'Connor is like Evelyn Waugh and J. F. Powers — but unlike most Catholic writers — in this: the ability to treat religious matters with humor.

Robert Lowell
 Poet

I loved and admired Flannery very much. She was one of the best writers in the country, a brave one, who never relaxed or wrote anything that didn't cost her everything. No one had her combination of humor and horror. Each story was as surely and meticulously written as the best short poems.

But I am afraid I haven't the leisure to write anything. I am up to my neck this fall in play rehearsals and teaching. I look forward to your Memorial number, and imagine that *Esprit* is one of the places where she would most like to be remembered, a place where her faith will be remembered and yet not used as an axe against the unbeliever.

Andrew Lytle
 Editor, "*The Sewanee Review*"

Years ago at Iowa City in a rather informal class meeting I read aloud a story by one of the students. I was told later that it was understood that I would know how to pronounce in good country idiom the word chitling which appeared in the story. At once it was obvious that the author of the story was herself not only Southern but exceptionally gifted. The idiom for her characters rang with all the truth of the real thing, but the real thing heightened. It resembled in tone and choice of words all country speech I had ever heard, but I couldn't quite place it. And then I realized that what she had done was what any first rate artist always does — she had made something more essential than life but resembling it. She had done this by the use of crucial words and the proper rhythm raised to a higher power. She was making her own language for the subject already seen to be uniquely her own.

This of course was Flannery O'Connor.

There is never any mistaking the authentic voice. And she had this voice if anybody ever did. She was from Georgia, because people in life and in fiction do not exist in a vacuum. The bad kind of provincial writing anywhere emphasizes costume and ornament, or the convention with no content. This is one definition of local color. But Miss O'Connor made formal by use of Southern manners and mores the subject central to Christendom in its imperilled plight in our time. The world now after a long decline of the order of Christendom is predominantly secular. The general enveloping action of her stories is a state not predominantly but absolutely secular and material, in which her heroes and heroines miss salvation because of complete selfishness and self-love. Actually it is impossible to find any society so given over totally to the evil nature of man. This can only be done in an art form. Hence the monstrosity and grotesqueness of her characters. Her action comes closer to allegory, but since her actors do not represent abstract qualities but enjoy the roundness of human kind, I would say that her fiction resembles more nearly a morality play. By showing the terrifying nature of a society entirely material and secular, with little or no relieving charity, she intended to shock, I think, us into an awareness of the present disguise the enemy of man now assumes.

She was courageous in her work, having to resist a mortal disease with a medicine no less dangerous, to which she finally succumbed. She was a young woman, but perhaps her work was done. One can admire her long fight against herself, so that her work might get done. The personal annihilation is the habit of all serious writers, to die in one way and be revived in another. So after all with Miss O'Connor we may grieve but not regret the greater intensity in her life and death of the artist's common plight.

Robie Macauley
Editor, "*The Kenyon Review*"

Her death is too recent and sadness too fresh for me to write anything very coherent about Flannery O'Connor. There is a particularly vivid feeling one has about gifted friends first known just when the gifts were beginning to appear. It is a feeling that always outlasts and outshines the milder friendships of later years. And so it is that almost everything Flannery wrote keeps a further, inexpressible meaning for me that other fiction does not have.

Most of Flannery's life must have been a torment. She wrote hard and re-wrote even more painfully; her terrible affliction was with her for many years. It is no wonder that her great subject was the anti-Christ — the fierce and bestial side of the human mind. She treated it with a confused and emotional hatred. The wonder is that she could express her hatred of ignorance so dryly, precisely, and penetratingly. I think that she could express it so only because she was so profoundly certain of the Good.

She knew the Good first and most importantly through her deep Catholic faith. Second, she knew it through a magnificent comic sense — a sense of humor that often comes out in her published work but which had an even greater freedom in her private letters. I have never known anyone whose wit had such edge and at the same time such kindness.

I must record one memory. One afternoon around 1949, we were sitting in the swing on the porch of Flannery's boarding house in Iowa City. We talked about the problem of Negroes and Whites in the South and wondered when and how the racial question would ever be settled. Flannery told an anecdote. She said that when John Crowe Ransom had been asked to read one of her stories before a writing class, he had suddenly come across the word "nigger." He refused to say it — all through the story he substituted "Negro" for "nigger." "It did spoil the story," Flannery said, "the people I was writing about would never use any other word. And Mr. Ransom knew that quite well. But he did the only thing a good man could do." It was a small incident, but I think that Flannery always knew, in her writing, that Christ is inward and, finally, inexpressible. The anti-Christ is present, visible, articulate; he walks around in the light of the sun. Her stories are mostly about him. And, she was saying, one must first know him before one can have a whole knowledge of Him.

Rev. Leonard F. X. Mayhew
Assoc. Ed., "*The Georgia Bulletin*"

" 'Yes'm,' The Misfit said as if he agreed. 'Jesus thrown everything off balance.' " Into this taut sentence from her short story "A Good Man Is Hard To Find" Flannery O'Connor crammed the major preoccupations of her rich and brilliant fiction. There is her concern for the South — with its uncomprehending and pathetic resistance to change, its colorful dialect, its apocalyptic religion. There is her hearty sense of the ironic. And, above all, there is the one "preoccupation" (that was her word) which outweighed all others: Christ and the still partial penetration of redemption into a lopsided world. In her note to the second edition of *Wise Blood* she gently rebuked those who had missed the point of her "comic novel": "That belief in Christ is to some a matter of no great consequence.

The critical mistake that most bedeviled her published work was to misread it as some neo-Gothic/neo-Virginia Woolf hybrid. Writing was difficult for her, she often confessed. It meant finding and following "every story needs a character who can do credibly." As a result, her "heroes" are grotesque and off-balance, precariously perched on the brink of hysteria. Her stories and her people are authentic and universal not because she realistically describes the outward experiences of herself and her community but because she pierces ruthlessly through this exterior shell to a common ground of human need, pain and expectation. She caught the sights and sounds of her world with breathtaking accuracy and vitality. But they have meaning only because she was able to transform them by her artistry.

The theme of Flannery O'Connor's fiction is free will. To her, this meant a struggle for identity, a conflict with the turmoil that has made itself at home in an unredeemed world and above all, in the part of ourselves that has stubbornly resisted redemption. "Free will does not mean one will, but many wills conflicting in one man. Freedom cannot be conceived simply. It is a mystery and one which a novel . . . can only be asked to deepen." Tarwater's compulsion, in *The Violent Bear It Away*, to baptize the idiot child and to preach in the city "the terrible speed of mercy" is neither false nor unfree. Its energy is grace and love. The violence, the grotesque imbalance, is in the "dark city where the children of God lay sleeping."

She compared her approach to reality and fiction to what the medieval doctors called the anagogical sense of Scripture, the real and intended significance embedded beneath the literal and empirical sense. Within this improbable-appearing world of her own creation, she wrote with the most delicate subtlety. Without a word of warning — and with no explicit reference to the theological insight which frames her thought — she withdraws us absolutely from the everyday world and we neither resist nor avert to the strenuous demands of the transfer. She leads us willingly into the otherwise incredible categories of her private Apocalypse. Under their façade of normalcy, she unveils the structure and relationships of daily experience as off-center and grotesque and violence-breeding. Caroline Gordon wrote of Flannery O'Connor's characters: "They are 'of-center', out of place, because they are victims of a rejection of the scheme of redemption. They are lost in that abyss which opens for man when he sets up as God."

Flannery O'Connor was widely held to be a "Catholic novelist," a term she professed not to understand. She prided herself on being "congenitally innocent of theory." In a real and special sense, however, she was precisely a "Catholic" novelist. She was very much aware of the presently effective currents in the Church. The title of her forthcoming collection of stories is from Teilhard de Chardin, "Everything that rises must converge." Her writing is profoundly marked by a highly individual synthesis of her Catholic philosophy with sympathy for the sometimes bizarre evangelism of the rural South. The religious mentality of free-wheeling preachers, self-anointed prophets and crucified lambs contained for her a kind of truncated sacramentalism. It sees the presence of the divine — of grace, if you will — immediately beyond the empirical and prosaic. Sunday supplements have made serpent handling, rolling, shouting and the mass hysteria of river baptism familiar. In this world the very experience of religious exaltation and ecstasy becomes a sacrament. Flannery O'Connor saw the people of this mentality as spiritual *emigrés* of the Old Testament, furiously digging and searching for real and operative sacraments. The outward signs they have at hand are recalcitrant and must be forced to reveal the salvation they contain. Only the violent may bear it away. Such souls are fertile ground, in her view, for divine mercy.

In addition, she was a Bible Belt Catholic, a member of a tiny minority. She felt the tension between loyalty to conviction and heritage on one hand, and the sense of alienation, of being irrevocably foreign and different, on the other. The priest in "The Displaced Person" is a naturally foreign figure in her world as well as a telling symbol for the purpose of the story.

The vision and mission of the prophet and seer are a staple of Flannery O'Connor's writing. Her characters' eyes are the symbol of that fearful vision: Tarwater's great uncle has "silver protruding eyes . . . like two fish straining to get out of a net of red threads;" Hazel Motes, vanquished, burns out his eyes. Truth — the living God — is a terrifying vision to be faced only by the stout of heart. Flannery O'Connor was such a seer, of stout heart and hope. From her loss we salvage the memory of a "stranger from that violent country where the silence is never broken except to shout the truth." May she rest.

Reprinted by permission of "Commonweal" magazine, (c) 1964.

Thomas Merton
Trappist Poet, Writer

We cannot well afford to lose as good a writer as Flannery O'Connor. To write so well in a society where everyone is literate is already a great thing: for where everyone reads and writes, everyone is banal. But Flannery O'Connor played expertly with the counterpoint of literacy and ignorance, cunning and absurdity, frankness and deceit, loneliness and connivance of sin. She made a subtle and dissonant, disturbing kind of Southern music. Full of irony and moral resonances, she avoided overt moral pronouncements with a consistency bordering on despair: the despair of goodness in men, whether of the country or of the city, of the old days or of today the "good man" is always "hard to find" and the innocent Bible salesman will steal a wise girl's artificial leg before you know where you are.

She was able to see all our failures and distortions mirrored in the more obvious madness of the South. She was at the same time completely disturbing and completely convincing. Sometimes her characters seemed incredible in their obsession, their cunning, their macabre wit, and it is precisely in their incredibility that the reader most firmly believes them. And this is the mark of a great artist. I will not call her pitiless: her reluctance to pronounce judgement or even to make a personal comment should be interpreted as a delicate form of compassion. Sometimes she writes of children who do not yet practice the wicked arts of maturity, and then she lets compassion for their loneliness be fully seen. But not all her children are unwise: their simplicity may endow them with a more direct and a more devastating maliciousness.

Flannery was great in her ear for the offbeat poetry of inane speech, her eye for the causal madness of irresponsibility, her grim pity for the obsessed and her tenderness toward those who are, (rarely), innocent. She had much to say that other writers could not tell us, and that is why she is such a loss. But once she is lost to us, then her art and her books must be better studied and meditated in fear and trembling. Her irony and compassion are above all to be remembered. They have a strange flavor, but once you have come to admit it as familiar, it cannot be forgotten.

Editor's note: We suggest you read Tho. Merton's prose eulogy in JUBILEE magazine, Nov., 1964.

J. Franklin Murray, S.J.
    Prof. Spring Hill College, Ala.

Christian authors have often written of the natural goodness of the human soul and of its affinity for the redemptive grace of Christ. They have further observed that the soul untouched by the grace of Baptism or deprived of it by repeated grave sin may become twisted, maimed, and hardened in evil. Some have contended that this distortion carries over into the body and that wicked men reflect their evil in their countenances and whole being. So thought Miss Flannery O'Connor, young Catholic author, who lived in rural Georgia and died there August 3. Miss O'Connor was a remarkably fine and talented person whose hobbies were painting and raising peacocks, but whose main work was writing vivid and witty short stories and novels about evil men and women who were twisted and maimed in soul and often in body. Some of her characters are grotesque, as in *Wise Blood* and *The Violent Bear It Away;* some are vicious and criminal as in her collection of short stories, *A Good Man is Hard To Find* and Other Stories.

The underlying theme of these refreshing works is that men are wicked and destructive because they are deprived of grace. They become maimed in their whole being because their natural affinity for sacramental grace is unsatisfied. They are left frustrated, evil, and incomplete.

In her short career of thirty-nine years, Miss O'Connor shed light and grace wherever she went and in whatever she wrote. She suffered much from the crippling disease of lupus, but she overcame her physical handicap with cheerfulness and courage. She was widely acclaimed and respected by scholars of all faiths and loved by all who knew her. Her lectures on literary theory and criticism were masterpieces of analysis, expressed with candor, economy, and vigor.

In a sense Miss O'Connor's life was a contradiction of much that she wrote, for she had a beautiful soul in an afflicted body. Her untimely death is a severe loss to Catholic writing. May her memory be blessed and her works endure as a monument to her talent.

William Van O'Connor
Editor, Critic, Writer, Prof. U. of Calif., Davis

Flannery O'Connor is one of the very few fiction writers today who are explicitly committed to Christian orthodoxy. Asked about the prevalence of grotesques in her novel and short stories, she said:

"I am not and have never been interested in the grotesque for its own sake or in freaks and abnormal people because of their freakishness or their abnormalities. It seems to me that the grotesque can have no meaning in fiction unless it is seen or felt in relation to what is right and normal. My own belief about what is (morally) right and normal comes from Christian orthodoxy; comes from believing that Christ should be the center of life and of the individual soul; whereas the most obvious thing about the society I live in and write about is that Christ is hardly the center of it. Even in the "Bible Belt" where I come from, Christ only haunts us from the fringes. I am a Catholic living in a society that is normally Protestant but isn't even that with much vigor any more. My angle of vision being what it is, I am probably conscious of many things as being grotesque, which people who are more a part of this society, more adjusted to it, would simply consider normal.

Also, I think that these are times when one who sees from a religious point of view will tend to certain violences of expression and form to get his vision across to what he will take to be a hostile audience. Writers who do believe in religious realities and propose to get them across in fiction have to cope with a deaf, dumb, and blind reader; and the grotesque may be one of our desperate answers."

Miss O'Connor's comment that "the grotesque may be one of our desperate answers" may help to explain the fanatical — one might almost say religious intensity, of her villains. She seems to be saying that fanatical villains are in desperate flight from God, or find in their own evilness a sense of significant being. In "A Good Man is Hard to Find" there is this curious exchange between The Misfit and the old lady he is getting ready to shoot, about the actions and teachings of Christ.

"No pleasure but meanness," he said, and his voice had become almost a snarl.

"Maybe He didn't raise the dead," the old lady mumbled, not knowing what she was saying and feeling so dizzy that she sank down in the ditch with her legs twisted under her.

"I wasn't there so I can't say He didn't" The Misfit said. "I wisht I had of been there," he said, hitting the ground with his fist. "It ain't right I wasn't there because if I had been I would of known. Listen, lady," he said in a high voice, "if I had of been there I would of known and I wouldn't be like I am now." His voice seemed about to crack and the grandmother's head cleared for an instant. She saw the man's face twisted close to her own as if he were going to cry and she murmured, "Why, you're one of my babies. You're one of my own children!" The Misfit sprang back as if a snake had bitten him and shot her three times through the chest. Then he put his gun down on the ground and took off his glasses and began to clean them.

> *"My own feeling is that the writers who see by the light of their Christian faith will have, in these times, the sharpest eyes for the grotesque, for the perverse, and for the unacceptable."*

"Good Country People" presents a character who loves his own viciousness with a gleeful, satanic intensity. The other leading character is a stout thirty-two year old girl. She had not had a normal life because she had a bad heart and in childhood had lost a leg. She had gone away to school and earned a Ph.D., then returned home. At twenty-one she had legally changed her name from Joy to Hulga, that being the ugliest name she could think of. Her only delights are her skepticism, cynicism, and sense of superiority over her mother and the townspeople. When a young Bible salesman comes to their house, Hulga decides to seduce him, a naive Bible salesman seeming an easy object for her perversity. She meets him in a hayloft. His guileless conversation causes her to feel a moment of selflessness, and she even allows him to remove her wooden leg. Finally understanding her sense of superiority he skillfully exploits it, and with equal skill humiliates her, finally going off with her wooden leg. 'And I'll tell you another thing, Hulga,' he said, using the name as if he didn't think much of it, 'you ain't so smart. I been believing in nothing since I was born!' and then the toast colored hat disappeared down the hole and the girl was left, sitting on the straw in the dusty sunlight."

Hazel Motes, the protagonist of *Wise Blood*, is Miss O'Connor's most desperate God-seeker. Brought up in a zealous household, with a fanatical grandfather who often said that Jesus would die ten million painful deaths even for him, a "mean, sinful unthinking boy." Hazel wants to be free from guilt, free from corruption. During his stay in the Army he is told he has no soul — which he has wanted to hear. Thereafter his unbelief is fanatical. Released from the Army, he preaches "the Church Without Christ," unmasks charlatans, and gives himself to whatever he had once thought to be sinful. In his fanatical contempt for dishonesty he kills one of the charlatans. But Hazel's journey toward unbelief is toward belief. In his self-hatred, he blinds himself. He lives a hermit's ascetic life, eating little, and punishing himself by walking on bits of glass and wrapping his body in barbed wire. His landlady, from whose perspective he is seen after what is apparently his reconversion, wonders what it is like to be blind.

> "How would he know if time was going backwards or forward or if he was going with it? She imagined it was like walking in a tunnel and all you could see was a pin point of light. She had to imagine the pin point of light; she couldn't think of it at all without that. She saw it as some kind of star, like the star on Christmas cards. She saw him going backwards to Bethlehem and she had to laugh."

Perversity is so prevalent in Miss O'Connor's stories that one reviewer has suggested a direct indebtedness to Poe. Her view on perversity, however, unlike Poe's, is related to Original Sin. There is nothing sentimental in her treatment of believers; sometimes they are stupid, and regularly they are willful and mean. Perversity is a part of the human condition. But Miss O'Connor sees Christian grace as ameliorating perversity. "A Temple of the Holy Ghost" has in it a self-centered sassy child who tries to overcome her faults. She is more than suffocated by a nun who likes to hug her, and she has her share of Hamlet's sense of this "too, too solid flesh." What troubles her most is the story she hears about a sideshow hermaphrodite having said, "I don't dispute it. This is the way He wanted me to be." And the child too learns not to "dispute it:" "She turned toward the window and looked over a stretch of pasture land that rose and fell with a gathering greenness until it touched the dark woods. The sun was a huge red ball like an elevated Host drenched in blood and when it sank out of sight, it left a line in the sky like a red clay road hanging over the trees." In "The Artificial Nigger" and "The River" the nature and function of grace are not merely described, they are dramatized; a child's soul is saved, even though he is physically lost, and an old man simultaneously sees his own monstrousness and feels the mercy of God.

But our thoroughly secularized world, Miss O'Connor is saying, does give perversity an added dimension in which to work. Her more fanatical villains are deeply aware of virtue and of religious belief, and take their stand against them. The lesser villains, like Mr. Shiftlet in "The Life You Save May Be Your Own," are likely to be merely lost in the great welter of chance relationships, with self-seeking and conniving dominating everything. These lesser villains often suffer from their sense that the "rottenness of the world (is) about to engulf" them.

It is not unfair to Miss O'Connor to say that the themes of her stories are for the most part straight out of the Catechism; they are about Original Sin, Christ's mercy, grace, repentance, and salvation. In what we tend to think of as the novels of sophisticated Catholic writers there is usually a special twist, for example, the Jansenist cast of mind in Mauriac or the paradox that pity destroys in Greene. Does Miss O'Connor's dependence on the Catechism sentimentalize her characters, make for a simplified black and white morality? None of her characters is sentimentalized, for she sees the potential evil in all human beings, and she is constantly aware of the incongruities in human actions. The answer to the other part of the question will in part depend on the orthodoxy or indifference to orthodoxy in the reader. "The River" is a Christian story and Hazel Motes is the Christian saint. We may observe that while T. S. Eliot's theology is often deplored, his poetry and plays which center in a religious quest are admired. At least one of his protagonists, Harry, is not unlike Hazel Motes.

Miss O'Connor has her special vision. She has introduced an older Christian tradition into Southern society, confronting two fairly separate mentalities: the "Bible Belt," and amoral modernism. In this context the old tradition is seen in strange juxtapositions, and it produces such grotesques as Hazel Motes and The Misfit.

William Peden
Writer, Prof. U. of Missouri

During the last decade of her brief career, Flannery O'Connor more and more clearly emerged as the most talented Southern woman writer since Eudora Welty, and *A Good Man Is Hard To Find*, 1955, is unquestionably one of the two or three most distinguished "first" collections of short stories since Miss Welty's *A Curtain of Green*. Following *A Good Man*, Miss O'Connor's talent deepened and widened, and such recent short stories as "Greenleaf," "Comforts of Home," and "Everything That Rises Must Converge" are among her very best work. It is some comfort, now that she is gone, to know that such shorter pieces and at least two unpublished stories found in manuscript at her death, will be collected and published early in 1965.

Flannery O'Connor's stories are compounded of compassion and cruelty, of the light and the dark, of the comic and the tragic. Such juxtaposition of what at first seem to be unreconcilable opposites had disturbed some of her critics who find her stated belief in orthodox religious values incompatible with her "black" humor and her preoccupation with violence and abnormality. The paradoxical nature of her short stories is not so confusing when one recalls the number and the function of the lame, the halt, and the blind, the freaks, derelicts, and rejects, of the Old and the New Testaments. In this light it becomes relatively simple to accept at face value Miss

O'Connor's statement that "writers who see by the light of their Christian faith will have, in these times the sharpest eyes for the grotesque, for the perverse and for the unacceptable." In these terms, it is not difficult to accept, similarly, her belief that in the greatest fiction, a writer's "moral sense coincides with his dramatic sense," nor does it come as any great shock to learn, as John Hawkes had told us, that she feels "more of a kinship with Hawthorne than with any other American writer" or that she admits to writing "what Hawthorne called 'romances'."

Miss O'Connor, in short, is essentially an allegorist or fantasist, as I have observed previously,[1] although her stories are so deeply anchored in specific time and place as to be as real as rain. In the highest sense she is an artist-moralist creating out of a traditional spiritual/ethical/religious dogma, not a journalist fumbling with Gothic monstrosities for their own sakes. Her eye is both upon this world and the next; here, again, we see her kinship with Hawthorne with whom she shares a deeply-committed concern for the abnormal, the diseased, and the bizarre.

The ultimate fault of her characters, Miss O'Connor's short fiction suggests, is primarily in themselves, not in their stars. Through arrogance, stupidity, or pride — and influenced, of course, by hereditary, environmental, and societal flaws — her people attempt to find *their own* salvation. By so doing they commit the cardinal sin of rejecting the redemptive function of Christianity; because of this rejection they wander through a dark world, lost, alone, or eventually destroyed.

> *"The novelist with Christian concerns will find in modern life distortions which are repugnant to him, and his problem will be to make these appear as distortions to an audience which is used to seeing them as natural . . . ."*

---

1. In *The American Short Story; Front Line In the National Defense of Literature*, 1964, published by Houghton Mifflin and used with permission of the publisher.

Laurence Perrine
Writer, Prof. Southern Methodist U.

Flannery O'Connor, for me, is enshrined in her short stories. It is a durable shrine, and needs no flowers laid by me at its base.

Let me instead pay brief tribute to the kindness, courage, and tart wit of the woman herself. I never met Miss O'Connor; but, presuming on a mutual friendship, I ventured to write her in the summer of 1964, asking questions about two of her stories. One question concerned "Greenleaf" (published in *The Kenyon Review* for Summer, 1956, and first prize winner in the O. Henry Awards for 1957). "Why is Mrs. May named Mrs. May ?" I asked. "The name Greenleaf is clearly symbolical, and therefore one also suspects some symbolical suggestion in the name May."

Miss O'Connor's reply, dated June 6, 1964, was written from a hospital in Atlanta, Georgia, a bare two months before her death. She answered, in a kindly letter that must have given her trouble to write at all, "As for Mrs. May, I must have named her that because I knew some English teacher would write and ask me why. I think you folks sometimes strain the soup too thin."

I still feel a pleasant ache where my wrist was thus lightly slapped by so gallant a lady.

J. F. Powers
Fiction Writer

Flannery O'Connor was an artist blessed (and cursed) with more than talent. In a dark and silly time, she had the great gift — the power and the burden — of striking fire and light. She was one of those rare ones, among writers, whose life's work was not in vain.

Orville Prescott
Critic, Writer, Editor

There are ten short stories in Flannery O'Connor's second book, *A Good Man Is Hard to Find*, and two of them are mediocre. The eight others are quite wonderful in a gruesome way and should confirm Miss O'Connor's claim to a high rank among our most talented younger writers. I haven't read anything that has impressed me more in several months. This young woman from Savannah, Ga., is an extraordinarily accomplished short-story writer. Her ability to bring a loathsome human specimen to repellent life is amazing. Her narrative power is exceptional in an era when so many gifted young writers scorn so elementary a virtue as storytelling. Her cold, precise, brutal style has the shocking power of a blow between the eyes. Her fictional world is a terrible one, but it is her own. Here is one young Southern writer who has something to say and the courage and good sense to say it in her own way without imitating anyone, least of all the literary sachem of Oxford, Miss.

Flannery O'Connor's first book, *Wise Blood*, was a novel about the lunatic fringe of religious fanaticism in the South. It made a lasting impression on many readers and critics. *A Good Man Is Hard to Find* is a collection of short stories about the least admirable human emotions — malice, fear, greed, hypocrisy, selfishness and cruelty. In every one of the ten stories these unpleasant aspects of human character are revealed as they are fostered and stimulated by ignorance.

Deeds of Degradation

Miss O'Connor's characters are not so far down the social and economic scale as the inhabitants of Erskine Caldwell's "Tobacco Road," but, to a man, they have pitifully narrow limitations. Miss O'Connor writes of them with sardonic humor and with contemptuous affection.

Most of these stories are laid in remote regions of rural Georgia. Most of them show people behaving despicably. The people are not only ignorant and spiteful. Some of them are feeble-minded, degraded and frighteningly malicious. Terrible things happen to them and they do terrible things to others. A psychopathic escaped convict murders a whole family. A young degenerate steals a cripple girl's artificial leg and leaves her isolated in the loft of a seldom-used barn. A one-armed tramp marries an idiot girl to steal her mother's fifteen-year-old jalopy. Miss O'Connor loves to conclude her stories on a note of grotesque horror.

But these are not mere horror stories told for the pleasure of making a reader's flesh creep. They are too close to the bedrock of human character to depend on the developments of their plots, no matter how arresting. These people live. Their stupid remarks, their wretched thoughts, their miserable conduct haunt the mind; Miss O'Connor impales them with a flashing phrase and holds them up, writhing, for inspection. One may shudder at the spectacle and flinch from such company, but one never feels that they are unreal or exaggerated for the sake of an artificial effect.

Mitigated by Pity

Such a collection of stark and savage tales might bludgeon readers into insensibility. But somehow Miss O'Connor never goes too far. Always she retains her sense of proportion and leavens her sordid situations with flashes of acid humor and with a feeling of human compassion. Only two of her characters are outright villains acting with consciously evil intent. All the others do what they do because they know no better, because they are doing what comes naturally to them. And a few are innocent victims of misfortune.

A more precise notion of the kind of fare to be found in *A Good Man Is Hard to Find* can best be given, I think, by indicating the situations described in the four stories that impressed me most. These are: "The River," which is about the neglected child of alcoholic parents, the ignorant woman hired to be his sitter who took him out for the day and what happened when she had the 4-year-old boy baptized in a river by a half-crazed, 19-year-old preacher and "healer"; "The Artificial Nigger," which is about an almost senile old man and a little boy lost in the streets of Atlanta, their different kinds of fear and the betrayals and reconciliations of their great adventure; "A Circle in the Fire," which is about the purposeless malice of three boys, an evil that is almost pitiful because it is mixed with an element of innocence; and "Good Country People," which is about a 32-year-old country girl with an artificial leg and a doctorate in philosophy and a 19-year-old Bible salesman who masks his depravity beneath an air of rustic virtue.

Obviously, *A Good Man Is Hard to Find* is not a dish to set before most readers. Those who are attracted by it will admire it immensely.

Orville Prescott
    "Books of The Times"

Flannery O'Connor, whose talent for fiction is so great as to be almost overwhelming, is a sort of literary white witch. She writes with blazing skill about the most appalling horrors and sometimes makes them seem entirely real and perfectly natural — major and inevitable elements in the sinful lot of man. But, according to an article Miss O'Connor wrote in "The Living Novel," a symposium edited by Granville Hicks, she brews her gruesome concoctions with the most exalted intentions. "A novelist with Christian concerns," Miss O'Connor called herself, who writes about what she sees in relation to "the Redemption of Christ." In Miss O'Connor's new novel, *The Violent Bear It Away*, that relationship is presumably present; but, if it is, it is not apparent to me. Nor do I think that it will be to many others.

On its surface, at least, *The Violent Bear It Away* is a novel about religious mania. It is written with all the dazzling verbal power that made Miss O'Connor's short stories unforgettable. The language is as original and striking. The intricate shifts in time and point of view are as deftly and unobtrusively contrived. The smooth rush of the narrative is as compelling. These are great virtues. But they are insufficient to atone for a grotesque and bizarre central situation that never seems real. One can pity Miss O'Connor's doomed characters as caricatured types of human misery; but one can't believe in them, or care about them.

Out of the Deep South

This is the story of four people: Francis Marion Tarwater, 14 years old, raised in a backwoods clearing somewhere in the Deep South by his great-uncle; the great-uncle, Mason Tarwater, 84, a distiller of moonshine whiskey who was called by the Lord to be His prophet and who was determined that the boy would succeed him even as Elisha succeeded Elijah; the boy's uncle, a kindly and well-intentioned school teacher named Rayber; and Rayber's idiot son, Bishop, 5 years old.

Old Tarwater, who had spent four years locked up in an insane asylum, is mad. His rantings, the only instruction the boy had ever received, had made him mad, too. So when the old man died and Tarwater (that's what he called himself) went out into the world to live with his uncle he went burdened with a mission. He knew that he had to take up the old man's prophetic mantle and that his first step must be to baptize the idiot child. The trouble was that Tarwater resented the domination under which he had lived and struggled against the compulsion which obsessed him.

So there was poor Tarwater, ignorant as a baby possum, stubborn as a Missouri mule, resentful and suspicious as a hound with a can tied to its tail, glaring at his baffled uncle, wrestling with his prophetic destiny, refusing any human contact. And there was his benevolent uncle, deaf, deserted by his wife, ineptly trying to befriend his sullen nephew and to enlighten his darkness with the teachings of modern science and psychology.

It was an impossible situation. But Miss O'Connor manages to get some harsh and sinister comedy out of it. Rayber never knew that Tarwater had to be a prophet and didn't want to be one. And the reader doesn't realize Tarwater's reluctance until too late for proper understanding. Probably it doesn't matter; any more than it matters that Tarwater and Rayber are mighty unconvincing specimens of opposing beliefs.

A Question of Faith

Since Tarwater's ideas of religion are identical with those of his mad great-uncle, complicated by some irrational fantasies of his own, they hardly seem adequate representatives of Christian faith, if that is what Miss O'Connor means them to be. And Rayber's bumbling, ineffectual trust in IQ tests and psychiatric theories is equally unsatisfactory if it is supposed to stand for modern scientific thought. There is considerable confusion here.

There also is a large dose of violence and horror. Tarwater, whose mind is only a murky darkness, commits a murder. It is supposed to be his great gesture of defiance against his prophetic destiny. And Tarwater is the victim of a brutal sexual assault, a monstrous misfortune which serves no purpose except to demonstrate Miss O'Connor's determination to pile horror upon horror. Consequently the wretched boy, always partly mad, becomes so completely mad that he sees signs and portents and interprets them as divine proofs that he must assume his prophetic destiny — a conclusion so arbitrary that it seems meaningless, just a neat way of making the wheel spin full circle.

Of course, in another novelist's hands such a conclusion might seem satirical and ironic. But not in Miss O'Connor's.

Sr. M. Bernetta Quinn, O. S. F.
Writer, Prof. College of St. Teresa. Minn.

Some years ago, through the kind offices of William Van O'Connor, then on the University of Minnesota staff and now in the English department of the University of California, Davis Branch, I was a contributor to an issue of *Critique* devoted to the talents of two brilliant young Catholic novelists, J. F. Powers and Flannery O'Connor. Few reactions to "appreciations" of this type have brought me the joy that Miss O'Connor's generous acknowledgement did, as expressed in a November 18, 1958 letter: "I suppose the greatest blessing a writer can have is a real reader, one who takes the pains to see what a story really does — as you have done." In the space since then, and especially following Miss O'Connor's death on August 3, 1964, articles on her have vividly revealed how many perceptive readers she had and has.

Student interest in Miss O'Connor's career increased steadily after the publication of her book of short stories *A Good Man Is Hard to Find*. By January, 1960, the College of Saint Teresa, Winona, Minnesota, had begun negotiations towards a three-day fiction workshop centering around Flannery O'Connor; to its extreme good fortune, such an event came about, despite the crippled condition which required her to walk with crutches. The opportunity occurred soon after the appearance of *The Violent Bear It Away*, an excursion into the deeper meanings of prophecy, a concept I hope to explore later in a longer essay relevant to Miss O'Connor's fictional use of it.

Correspondence planning for the visit to the Winona campus includes this sentence from the author concerning her second novel: "Those who, like Tarwater, see, will see what they have no desire to see and the vision will be the purifying fire." This artistic fascination with prophecy had begun as early as *Wise Blood* (1952), with its unforgettable hero Hazel Motes. Like the hazel wand in William Butler Yeats, this hero has a supernatural character, his actions leading to happenings understandable only in terms of the implications of the Redemption.

The next October brought Miss O'Connor to Minneapolis by plane — the only way her disability enabled her to travel — where Teresan faculty members met her and drove her to the College for the fiction-workshop, with its marginal activities. Thus began a most wonderful experience, between October 17 and 19, both for the college students and the faculty. Miss O'Connor's spontaneous feeling for people made the time one of giving: a convocation, a fifteen-minute radio interview, a creative writing seminar (with students present from the nearby Saint Mary's College for men), meetings with underdivision classes, a session with the staff members of the literary quarterly, and several informal discussions, over meals and elsewhere, on fiction.

What Miss O'Connor said — on the auditorium stage, in the South Lounge seminar gathering, in her delightfully comic and wise conversation with the three student-journalists recorded in the Fall, 1960 *Censer*, then moderated by poet William Goodreau — meant something very special to each auditor. But it was her *self*, the complete honesty combined with just the right degree of kindness, which will always be the treasured memory of those who shared her stay in Winona that fall. She later also spoke while in Minnesota at the College of Saint Catherine in Saint Paul and at the University of Minnesota Newman Club, before boarding the plane once more, fortified with a box of fudge made by one of the Franciscan Sisters as a gift to Miss O'Connor's mother. The simplicity of the guest can be illustrated by a line from the letter she sent back on October 22, after her return to Milledgeville, Georgia: "It meant a great deal to me to come to Saint Teresa's."

From Milledgeville the next spring came an account of Flannery's surprised reaction to the news that a publisher had actually accepted the biography of Mary Ann, a book written by two Sisters in an Atlanta, Georgia hospital where the novelist had formerly been a patient. Mary Ann had died joyously and bravely at twelve, her ailment cancer of the face. Having refused to do the biography herself since she felt unqualified in this *genre* (she was realistic about her limitations), Miss O'Connor had prepared a lengthy introduction to the book which undoubtedly played a large role in its acceptance. About the acceptance she wrote: "I had bet the Sisters a pair of peacocks that nobody would ever buy it, so week before last they came down to pick up the peafowl in their station wagon. They built a house and a seventy-five foot run for them and they say the patients who can get out just sit and look at them."

Sister Emmanuel Collins, Dean of the College of Saint Teresa, and Miss O'Connor were both awarded honorary degrees in June of 1963 at Saint Mary's College in South Bend, Indiana. Later that year, Flannery wrote back to CST that she had received a similar degree from Smith College. "It was wholesale day," she commented; "there were six of us." That summer had forced upon her the hard decision of limiting to an absolute minimum her absences from Milledgeville, both because of health difficulties and in order not to interfere with her writing.

In the autumn of 1963, Miss O'Connor achieved two short stories, a feat which she labeled "phenomenal output for me. However, when they come, they come, and when they don't, they don't — though you have to work at it every day." Even during her last illness she continued to work at her fiction, describing herself as hopping from the bed to the electric typewriter, like a bird from nest to limb.

The disease which was Miss O'Connor's outstanding cross — though her matter-of-factness would have considered this way of putting it pretentious — grew rapidly worse, though with periods of improvement. On January 25, 1964 she wrote: "I'm feeling a lot better this past week and am almost back to working full time — full time is three hours a day. I'm not sure just what happens to the others."

In August of that year Flannery O'Connor died at thirty-nine. The Most Reverend Paul Halliman, Archbishop of Atlanta, concluded in these words his tribute to her in *The Georgia Bulletin:* Our South and our Church are poorer because of the death of a fine young writer. But we are confident that the Judgement degrees include the artist as well as the mother, the nurse, the worker in social needs. "Whatever you did for the least of these, you did for Me."

May God grant her eternal light and life, the reflection of which was her great contribution to our world.

The temporal phase of Miss O'Connor's life is fittingly described by the term "design in courage." If one looks deeply into what she wrote, the same courage will there be evident, a courage facing life as it is while at the same time believing in that metamorphosis which Redemption can effect.

> *"Those who believe that art proceeds from a healthy, and not from a diseased, faculty of the mind will take what the artist shows them as a revelation, not of what we ought to be but of what we are at a given time and under given circumstances; that is, as a limited revelation but a revelation nevertheless."*

Louis D. Rubin
Writer, Critic, Prof.

Flannery O'Connor was a quiet, pleasant, humorous young woman, very much a Georgian and very folksy in her manner, who wrote some of the most unpleasant and grim fiction ever written. Anyone who knew the fiction first, and subsequently met Flannery, had difficulty in believing that this unobtrusive, gentle lady could have written such stories as "The Life You Save May Be Your Own." But she did, and many another powerful and savage story about the world she knew and imagined, and her early death was a deprivation for us all.

As had often been said, Flannery was a Southern writer and a Catholic writer, and these two apparently incongruous literary attitudes were combined in her fiction in a quite distinctive way. The texture of her work, the dialogue, the setting, the people, places and activities, were Southern. They were somewhat reminiscent of the fiction of Erskine Caldwell, though I hasten to add that unlike Caldwell she never exploited people or subordinated artistic observation for pruriency or sensation. But both Georgia writers shared a taste for depicting the grotesque and the ludicrous in the pathetic lives of farm folk and villagers living without the light. Underlying this Southern texture, however, was a moral structure, a pattern and development, formed along religious lines, so that all her work has for its form the drama of salvation.

Each of these literary modes complemented the other; her moral purposes never drifted into allegory, and at all times remained fixed in the meaning, never becoming overt in the texture. She was thus that rare specimen, a consciously and intentionally religious writer who never confused fiction and homiletics. There is in her fiction no hint of condescension, no smug looking down at the foibles and gropings of poor unfortunates living without the Word. She took her people with absolute seriousness; she gave them dignity and importance.

She was a humorist, essentially; her work is filled with irony and wit. She had a fine ear for dialogue, she enjoyed chronicling the outrageous, the incongruous. But the humor is not slapstick or flippant; it arises out of the discrepancy between human limitations and aspirations, and is essentially compassionate. Her people are unfulfilled because they are starved for emotional and spiritual fulfillment.

Once at a meeting of Southern writers she was asked how she felt, as a Southerner, to be writing in the shadow of William Faulkner. "Well," she drawled, "nobody likes to get caught on the tracks when the Dixie Flyer comes through." But of course she did not write in the shadow of Faulkner, or of anyone else. She was quite original, and her work was unmistakably her own.

For so very feminine and charming a person, her work always seemed to me to be highly masculine and unfeminine. A writer such as Eudora Welty, for example, is a very feminine writer; no one would ever think that anyone but a woman had written a book such as *Delta Wedding* or *The Golden Apples*. Not so with Flannery O'Connor's work;

it is hard, dramatic, desperate, and makes no concessions.

Like many others, I feel that it was as a short story writer that Flannery O'Connor was at her best. Much though I admire elements of *Wise Blood* and *The Violent Bear It Away*, neither of these longer works quite comes off. Perhaps it is because she is so very intense a writer that only her short stories can bear the weight of that concentration of form and meaning she brought to the craft of fiction. In any event, some of the stories seem to me quite flawless. To create perfect short fiction is an art that few have mastered; Flannery O'Connor did it again and again.

Philip Scharper
  Sr. Ed., Sheed & Ward

Flannery O'Connor was one of those artists — rare in any age — who saw life *sub specie aeternitatis*. The world she created in her fiction is a world constantly open to gleams from that other, more enduring world in which she believed both as a person and as an artist. Her characters move in the presence of grace, and God, although unseen and silent, is an actor in her dramas.

This, I think, is one clue to understanding Miss O'Connor's work, and one measure of her achievement. She *assumes* God and grace; they are among the givens of her work and hence she has not need — as lesser religious writers do — to argue their presence or violently to introduce them.

As a consequence of her Christian vision, Miss O'Connor was able to create a world which, in its complexity, mirrors faithfully the complexity of the Christian life.

It is a world, for example, where choice as an Apostle does not guard one against his own folly, as Peter came bitterly to learn; daily intimacy with the Son of God made possible the ultimate treason, as Judas demonstrates.

It is a world teeming with possibilities, wherein the opening of a door may have eternal consequences, or merely admit the delivery boy. It is a world charged with contradiction and paradox: we all know (and Miss O'Connor's characters know) the stricken cry of St. Paul when he marvelled that he did not the good which he wanted, and did the evil that he wanted not.

It is her sense of complexity, her realization that life is a crucible in which souls are made or broken, that gives to Miss O'Connor's work the quality of compassion. Her characters — often "grotesque" as Dostoevsi's characters were — seem, in their twisted being, larger than life because they are projected against the screen of eternity. But this magnification does not have the effect of making moral evil seem overwhelming (as often in Faulkner) but rather shows us that evil can be overcome only by Good.

A sense of complexity, a quality of compassion. These are unusual enough in the fiction of any age; they are all but absent in our own. Perhaps this is why one feels that in the untimely death of Flannery O'Connor the voice of an unearthly wisdom has been stilled while yet we had so much more to learn from her.

Nathan A. Scott, Jr.
Critic, Writer, Prof. U. of Chicago

I never had the good fortune to meet Flannery O'Connor, and the closest I ever came to getting a sense of her actual personality was by way of an account of a visit paid her a few years ago by a student of mine who, while spending a Christmas holiday in Atlanta, rang her up one day on the telephone to ask if he could come out to Milledgeville, and to whom she was wonderfully kind through a whole afternoon and evening. Yet, though never having known her personally, I — like many others, I imagine — was stung by a sense of loss and by a great sadness, when, on the morning following her death last August, I first learned of it from the obituary notice in the *New York Times*. One had known of her valiant struggle with the painful and crippling disease from which she had so long suffered; and one felt that, in bringing release from all that, her death had been something of a blessing. But, even so, one was filled with regret, for the wit and playfulness and *esprit* that had so brilliantly marked her fiction had come to suggest the qualities of spirit by which, as one imagined, this remarkable young woman managed somehow, finally, to prevail over the frailty of her body: so one felt that, had she been permitted a decision in the matter, she would probably have chosen to go on; and thus one wished that she might have been able to do so, even at a great cost. For, as a writer, hers was a very considerable gift, and she had *added* to the furniture of the American imagination, as only genius can.

One also hopes, now that her voice is stilled, that her work will begin to be freshly appreciated, and at a deeper level than that at which many of her interpreters have rested. A few of her critics occasionally, it is true, have perceived her trenchancy and seriousness. But far too many have been content to tuck her work away under some such foolish rubric as "Southern Gothic"; and thus, as the notion has gained currency that hers is the same vein as *Tobacco Road* and *Baby Doll* and *Other Voices, Other Rooms*, many of her readers have failed to grasp the radical kinds of moral judgment into the service of which Flannery O'Connor was intent on putting her art. It was indeed always an art that very much wanted to wake the spirit's sleep, to break that somnolence into which we flee from the exactions of the moral life. One thinks, for example, of that holy fool who is at the center of *Wise Blood* (1952), the young preacher of the Church Without Christ, Haze Motes, who proclaims the gospel of "no truth behind all truths." This self-ordained backwoods evangelist of an hysterical nihilism lives in darkness: yet, amidst this darkness, he is a "pinpoint of light," whose grotesque extremism of speech and behavior provides a deeply ironical measure of what is really heretical in the smug philistinism represented by both the conventional heretics and the conventional believers. And it is something like the same conclusion towards which we are brought by the book of 1960, *The Violent Bear It Away*, and by many of the stories. It is, to be sure, an art that found its chief materials in the grotesque and the deformed, and in the remote backwaters of the Southern Bible Belt. But, like the Hardy of the Wessex novels and the Faulkner of Yoknapatawpha county, she knew how to turn the very remoteness of her scene to advantage; and, however *outre* may be the crankiness of her *dramatis personae*, if we look hard enough, we can find in the very crookedness of their aberrancy what she called "the lines that create spiritual motion."

The cruel fate which struck this gifted young woman down before her fortieth birthday kept her, unfortunately then, from producing a large body of work; but, when her last book — *Everything That Rises Must Converge* (the title being drawn from Pere Teilhard de Chardin) — is published early in 1965, she will have given us (along with *Wise Blood* and *A Good Man Is Hard To Find* and *The Violent Bear It Away*) four books which are to be counted amongst the finest fiction produced anywhere by her literary generation. And not least remarkable is that hers is a body of work made rich and radiant by a Christian presence whose authenticity we are only just now at last beginning to discern.

So it is hoped that in the next few years we shall not slacken in trying to learn how to value more truly and to love more deeply the good legacy of Mary Flannery O'Connor, departed this life on the third day of August, 1964.

Ted R. Spivey
Critic, Writer, Prof. Ga. State College

One hears often about writers who are spokesmen for youth. Like all true artists Flannery O'Connor was a spokesman for God, but in her best work she was also a speaker to youth. In the stories and novels she left us Miss O'Connor spoke, and of course still speaks, to youth not so much as one who voices their agonies and their joys, although she does this too, but as one who in her fiction asks and answers questions about God and man that young people are once again pondering. How Miss O'Connor's work speaks to youth can be approached from the standpoint of her connection with another Georgia writer with whom she is often compared — Carson McCullers. The basic viewpoints of the two are quite different. Miss McCullers is a popular and sometimes powerful spokesman for youth, but Flannery O'Connor speaks as a leader who points out new paths of discovery. In this light the meaning of her work is only beginning to be understood. Today spokesmen are still preferred to speakers, or leaders, but tomorrow may be different.

With works like *The Heart is a Lonely Hunter* and *The Member of the Wedding* Carson McCullers occupies today a major place in a movement which still has no official literary label but which, for lack of a better name, might be called the school of the sensitive outsider. J. D. Salinger is, in the minds of many, the leading figure of this group, whose writing deals with misunderstood young people lost in a confusing world and often destroyed by this world and by their own neuroses. The protagonists in the fiction of this school are usually to be found, at the end of a story or novel, wandering aimlessly. But Miss O'Connor is always drawing her protagonists into man's most profound quest: the search for God. The basic difference between the work of the writers of the school of the sensitive outsider and that of Flannery O'Connor is intellectual background. The thinking that lies behind the work of Salinger and McCullers is a vague humanitarianism and, in the case of Salinger's more recent work, an equally vague religiosity. The intellectual basis of Miss O'Connor's work is theology.

Miss O'Connor is unquestionably a religious writer in the tradition of Bernanos and Mauriac. She spoke more than once of her debt to these two Frenchmen. Like them she does not put her characters into an intellectual and theological mold as second-rate writers often do. As an artist she works as all true artists must. With a grace no man can analyze she has created living fictional images which point toward basic truths and the mystery that surrounds creation. In her case the truths were and are theological. Like Mauriac and Bernanos she has demonstrated that a writer can retain orthodox beliefs and still be an artist. This was not hard to do in earlier centuries but today it is something so rarely seen that some people doubt that it can be done at all. Miss O'Connor herself had this to say of her work in an interview printed in 1962 in *The Saturday Review* in which she told Granville Hicks: " 'I'm not interested in the sects as sects; I'm concerned with the religious individual, the backwoods prophet.' "   The writer, if he is to be artist rather than preacher or propagandist, must begin with the heart and soul of man. But the greatest artists have shown man reaching out not only to his brothers but to God and to the truth about God. From her first novel, *Wise Blood,* to the sketch called *Why Do the Heathen Rage* printed in *Esquire* in 1963, which was part of a novel she was writing when she died, Miss O'Connor depicts passionate individuals reaching out to God and trying to know better the truths about God.

There is every indication that today young people are deserting the old humanitarian ideas — the political and social problems and solutions with which their parents were concerned. The fiction of Flannery O'Connor speaks very directly to people who still are having trouble believing that theology is central to man's concerns. The great increase of interest in Existential philosophy since World War II is one indication of youth's concern with searching out new paths to follow. As the atheistic Existentialism of Sartre and Camus has come to seem less exciting with the passage of time, so the theological Existentialism of Tillich, Marcel, Buber and others has come to occupy the minds of young people. Camus, for example, is valuable as a critic of a world without God, but his criticism of secular humanitarianism as a way of life in his novel *The Fall* is equalled or possibly excelled by Miss O'Connor in *The Violent Bear It Away* and *The Lame Shall Enter First*. But whereas Camus leaves his protagonist in *The Fall* sunk in dejection, Miss O'Connor depicts the struggle of men to get out of the hole into which secular humanitarianism had led man.

Along with the discovery of Existential theology has come the discovery that authors like Dostoevski and Kafka wrote a kind of Existential theology as a part of their best fiction. William Barrett in *Irrational Man* correctly sums up the basic ideas of religious Existentialism: "What is common and central to all these philosophers [the religious Existentialists] is that the meaning of religion, and religious faith, is recast in relation to the individual." This quotation is one way of defining what Flannery O'Connor was doing in her work: relating religious faith to the struggle to find God. Like Dostoevski Miss O'Connor deals with the criminal, the man separated from society because of his violence. The Misfit and Tarwater, two of her most memorable characters, are at war with themselves and with society; but they know how to ask the right questions and the very intensity of their desire to know is a sign itself to a new generation of young people who more than ever before want to hear not so much an echo of their own voices as the voice of one who has trod difficult paths and has something to report. Flannery O'Connor was such a person and her best protagonists, who I believe will live long in the minds and hearts of many people, were such individuals.

I cannot at this time, so soon after her death, write about Flannery O'Connor without saying something about the kind of person she was. She and I were natives of the same section of Georgia; and in our conversations and letters, which I am sad to say extended over a period of only six years, we often talked of our native heath as, of all Americans, only Southerners can. We also spoke of religion and of God; my Protestantism and her Catholicism in no way inhibited our dialogue. We read many of the same books and loved many of the same authors, and we had our intellectual differences, which we often made known to each other. It is hard for me to believe that another writer of our time could give as much of himself as she gave to people. In a time when most artists and intellectuals withdraw from the deeper kinds of personal relationship, she and her mother, Mrs. Regina O'Connor, were welcoming people of all persuasions and views — writers, scholars, businessmen, priests, farmers, doctors — to their lovely home standing in the rolling hills north of Milledgeville. I think Flannery might have been one of those writers of whom one could say it was even better to have known the person than to have read the work. And I have a very high regard for her work. In fact, as a teacher of literature. I throw away the usual caution of the scholar and say that in my opinion she is the most important writer America has produced since World War II. But when I think of her as a writer, I must also think of the mind and the heart and the soul of a woman who was a lady, an artist, and a Christian.

Allen Tate
  Critic, Poet, Writer, Prof. U. of Minn.

  I never knew Flannery O'Connor well, having met her only twice; first at the University of Iowa, I believe in 1947, where she was a student in the Writers' Workshop and I was the visiting writer whose job was to "criticize" the work of the young writers in the week I was there; and second, I saw her again in 1949 or 1950 in Connecticut, where she was staying at the country house of Robert and Sally Fitzgerald. The Fitzgeralds had made her a member of the family, and the role of niece or younger sister suited her very well. At that time I was not well acquainted with her work: I knew only a few short stories, and the fragment of *Wise Blood* that I had read at Iowa in 1947.

  And how irrelevant my remarks on *Wise Blood* must have seemed to her! I hadn't the vaguest idea of what she was up to; I offered to correct her grammar; I even told her that her style was dull, the sentences being flat and simple declaratives. No doubt what I said was true; but it was irrelevant. The flat style, the cranky grammar, the monotonous sentence-structure were necessary vehicles of her vision of man. It was a narrow vision, but deep; unworldly, but aware of human depravity as only a good Jansenist can be (by "good Jansenist" I mean only that Flannery took a gloomy view of the human condition and that all her characters, like Mauriac's, are possibly damned. Her characters resist grace, there is no free will, etc. She was not doctrinally but temperamentally a Jansenist — Again, by "good" I mean *thorough*); yet compassionate towards all the maimed souls she put into her stories. I didn't know these things when I saw her in Iowa. I only read "Good Country People," the first story of hers that I remember reading. Hulga, the girl with a wooden leg, is also spiritually maimed but she is still capable of love, even if, at the moment she thinks she is being seduced by the Bible salesman, she can see no further than physical love. The Bible salesman himself — who represents for Hulga's mother "good country people" — is a moral monster without human motivation even towards evil: he is *evil*. I would guess that all Miss O'Connor's stories are set in motion by such persons; for although the surface action is naturalistic, it is not possible to determine *why* the action starts, unless one posits a non-rational (not-rational) principle of supernatural disorder underlying the movement towards the destruction of the central characters. Her stories exhibit, either in the title or in the situation out of which the action begins, a *moral platitude*: Hulga's mother receives the Bible salesman because he is a good country boy trying to get ahead by means of the pious work of selling Bibles: the climax of the story explodes the platitude. The characters speak nothing but platitudes, and when evil has done its work with the platitudes the result is a powerful irony which, though crudely violent, is inherent in the situation, not laid on as commentary by the author.

I have frequently wondered what sort of writer Flannery would have been had she lived all her life in a Catholic community. In Milledgeville, Georgia, one would surmise, the population is about one percent Catholic. She was a Catholic necessarily writing about Protestants — and they all are decadent Protestants. Are there any Protestants at all in J. F. Powers' stories? I can't remember any. The unusual combination of Southern gentry with Roman Catholicism gave Flannery O'Connor a unique point of view. This, with her inexplicable genius, produced a writer whose like probably will not appear again in the United States.

Robert Penn Warren
Writer, Novelist, Critic, Prof. Yale

Flannery O'Connor had a subtle and beautifully equilibrated intelligence and an eye that missed nothing, the twist of a mouth, the light on a leaf. Her imagination often saw actuality as exploding into — or bleeding into — the fantastic and the macabre, but that imagination was so strongly geared to the inner logic of experience that her fantasy comes to us as a form of truth. She is original. She is sometimes spoken of as a member of the "Southern school" (whatever that is), but she is clearly and authoritatively herself, and she will, no doubt, speak in her special tone to many people for a very long time to come. She will give them her own kind of pleasure —glittering, painful, redemptive. In other words, she is that rare thing: an artist.

I never saw Flannery O'Connor but once, when, some years ago, we were guests in the same house in Tennessee, for a couple of days. I found her witty, shrewd, and strangely serene; for you had the sense that she loved the world and even forgave nonsense, not too tardily. Some time later she sent my little girl, whom she had never seen, a bright piece of a peacock's tail.

Joel Wells
Editor, "The Critic"

She was among the very best American short story writers of the last twenty-five years but everything she wanted to say was in her novel *The Violent Bear It Away*. I only met her twice and can't claim to have known her well but even those few hours were enough to make a lasting impression. She had a quality which Katherine Anne Porter described in a letter in which she agreed to write an appreciation of Miss O'Connor for our magazine: "She was a genius, no doubt of that . . . by what means she came to it so early I do not know, but she was at the center of the vortex — the great stillness that comes of tensions balanced against each other until perfect equilibrium is reached."

Besides all this she had a marvelous wit and a warm sense of humor which lights many of her short stories. As Truman Capote wrote of her: "She has some wonderful moments, that girl." Now that "has" must be read as past tense but it is true in the broadest sense. Her work, all of it, will last.

Eudora Welty
Novelist

In her cruelly short life, Flannery O'Connor wrote novels and stories whose distinguishing mark, to me, is their triumphant vitality. Her work speaks steadily of an exuberance of spirit, and straight out of this, it seemed, came the joyous command she always had of a talent of great lights and darks. She wrote with deep commitment about what put the greatest demands on her, and achieved a fiction of originality and power. Her concern was of course with the spirit, which in her stories made for richness with many faces. And I shall always treasure for my particular love and admiration her comic gifts. Work as good as hers makes all writers proud.

Ray B. West, Jr.
Critic, Prof. San Francisco State College

Flannery O'Connor saw the world as something that to most eyes would appear a distorted, even grotesque, image. What it represented was, in truth, a fresh vision — a penetration into the heart of the human condition in our time. With Miss O'Connor gone our own vision remains blurred, but still a little sharper than it was before. Hers was an untimely death, not just because she died so young, but because we are yet so much in need of her unique talent.

Miss O'Connor's quotations are from her essay in "The Living Novel," ed. Granville Hicks, (c) 1957, and used with permission of The Macmillan Co., N.Y.

Gracious Greatness
KATHERINE ANNE PORTER

ESPRIT expresses its special gratitude to Miss Porter for telephoning — from her sick bed in her Washington home — the following reminiscence of Miss O'Connor.

I saw our lovely and gifted FLANNERY O'CONNOR only three times over a period, I think, of three years or more, but each meeting was spontaneously an occasion and I want to write about her just as she impressed me.

I want to tell what she looked like and how she carried herself and how she sounded standing balanced lightly on her aluminum crutches, whistling to her peacock who came floating and rustling to her, calling in their rusty voices.

I do not want to speak of her work because we all know what is was and we don't need to say what we think about it but to read and understand what she was trying to tell us.

Now and again there hovers on the margin of the future a presence that one feels as imminent — if I may use stylish vocabulary. She came up among us like a presence, a carrier of a gift not to be disputed but welcomed. She lived among us like a presence and went away early, leaving her harvest perhaps not yet all together gathered, though, like so many geniuses who have small time in this world, I think she had her warning and accepted it and did her work even if we all would like to have had her stay on forever and do more.

It is all very well for those who are left to console themselves. She said what she had to say; I'm pretty certain that her work was finished. We shouldn't mourn for her but ourselves and our loves.

After all, I saw her just twice — memory has counted it three — for the second time was a day-long affair at a Conference and a party given by Flannery's mother in the evening. And I want to tell you something I think is amusing because Flannery lived in such an old-fashioned southern village very celebrated in southern history on account of what took place during the War. But in the lovely, old, aerie, tall country house and the life of a young girl living with her mother in a country town so that there was almost no way for her knowing the difficulties of human beings and her general knowledge of this was really very impressive because she was so very young and you wondered where — how — she had learned all that. But this is a question that everybody always asks himself about genius. I want to just tell something to illustrate the southern custom.

Ladies in Society there — that particular society, I mean — were nearly always known, no matter if they were married once or twice, they were known to their dying day by their maiden names. They were called "Miss Mary" or whoever it was. And so, Flannery's mother, too; her maiden name was Regina Cline and so she was still known as "Miss Regina Cline" and one evening at a party when I was there after the Conference, someone mentioned Flannery's name and another — a neighbor, mind you, who had probably been around there all her life — said, "Who is Flannery O'Connor? I keep hearing about her." The other one said, "Oh, you know! Why, that's Regina Cline's daughter: that little girl who writes." And that was the atmosphere in which her genius developed and her life was lived and her work was done. I myself think it was a very healthy, good atmosphere because nobody got in her way, nobody tried to interfere with her or direct her and she lived easily and simply and in her own atmosphere and her own way of thinking. I believe this is the best possible way for a genius to live. I think that they're too often tortured by this world and when people discover that someone has a gift, they all come with their claws out, trying to snatch something of it, trying to share some thing they have no right even to touch. And she was safe from that: she had a mother who really took care of her. And I just think that's something we ought to mention, ought to speak of.

She managed to mix, somehow, two very different kinds of chickens and produced a bird hitherto unseen in this world. I asked her if she were going to send it to the County Fair. "I might, but first I must find a name for it. You name it!" she said. I thought of it many times but no fitting name for that creature ever occurred to me. And no fitting word now occurs to me to describe her stories, her particular style, her view of life, but I know its greatness and I see it — and see that it was one of the great gifts of our times.

I want to speak a little of her religious life though it was very sacred and quiet. She was as reserved about it as any saint. When I first met her, she and her mother were about to go for a seventeen day trip to Lourdes. I said, "Oh, I wish I could go with you!" She said, "I wish you could. But I'll write you a letter." She never wrote that letter. She just sent a post card and she wrote: "The sight of Faith and affliction joined in prayer — very impressive." That was all.

In some newspaper notice of her death mention of her self-portrait with her favorite peacock was made. It spoke of her plain features. She had unusual features but they were anything but plain. I saw that portrait in her home and she had not flattered herself. The portrait does have her features, in a way, but here's something else. She had a young softness and gentleness of face and expression. The look — something in the depth of the eyes and the fixed mouth, the whole pose fiercely intent — gives an uncompromising glimpse of her character. Something you might not see on first or even second glance in that tenderly fresh-colored, young, smiling face; something she saw in herself, knew about herself, that she was trying to tell us in a way less personal, yet more vivid than words.

The portrait, I'm trying to say, looked like the girl who wrote those blood-curdling stories about human evil — NOT the living Flannery, whistling to her peacocks, showing off her delightfully freakish breed of chickens.

I want to thank you for giving me the opportunity to tell you about the Flannery O'Connor I know. I loved and valued her dearly, her work and her strange unworldly radiance of spirit in a human being so intelligent and so undeceived by the appearance of things. I would feel too badly if I did not honor myself by saying a word in her honor: it is a great loss.

SHORT STORY

I.   Contest
II. Symposium
III. The Regional Writer

SHORT STORY

I. CONTEST

Milledgeville
Georgia
28 February 58

Father Quinn
Esprit
University of Scranton
Scranton, Pennsylvania

Dear Father Quinn:

I enclose the stories. They are all pretty awful but I suppose this is only what you can expect from undergraduates writing fiction for the first time. Fiction writing requires more that just a way with words and I don't believe that most people of eighteen and nineteen and twenty have the maturity to cope with it. However, if they want to write it, they have to start sometime and they can learn from these early efforts.

Here it is a matter of deciding which is least bad, and a great strain it is; but my vote will have to go to the one called THE DAY HE DIED, because it has more of the elements of fiction in it that the other three, which are not much more than anecdotes. I feel that THE DAY HE DIED at least sets out to be a story. There is more effort in it, more possibility, some sense of characters moving in a meaningful situation, some sense of place. (It's still pretty bad.) My advice would be to take that ten dollars and buy each of these lads a copy of Brooks and Warren's UNDERSTANDING FICTION.

As for ranking the others, that is almost impossible. They all three sound a little like the Rover Boys trying to write a Mickey Spillane story. The one called THE THIEF has some striking images in it here and there; the one called THE HARD LUCK STORY has a good consistency of tone; and I am struggling hard to think of something good to say about the other one. Well, the boy is only a freshman. I am forced to recall that the stories I wrote when I was this age were no better than these.

I wish you the best with the magazine and I hope I have not been too depressing a judge. You may have a lot of potential talent in these boys, but at their age it's all guesswork.

Sincerely,
Flannery O'Connor

II. SYMPOSIUM

FLANNERY O'CONNOR

This perceptive, Southern writer has published in quality magazines, especially The Kenyon Review; in fact, Miss O'Connor has been awarded the Kenyon Fellowship. The result is A GOOD MAN IS HARD TO FIND, her collection of short stories. She has also published a novel, WISE BLOOD. Her new novel, THE VIOLENT BEAR IT AWAY, will be published in February, 1960.

Q: What is a short story?
1. This is a hellish question inspired by the devil who tempts textbook publishers. I have been writing stories for fifteen years without a definition of one. The best I can do is tell you what a story is not.
    1) It is not a joke.
    2) It is not an anecdote.
    3) It is not a lyric rhapsody in prose.
    4) It is not a case history.
    5) It is not a reported incident.

It is none of these things because it has an extra dimension and I think this extra dimension comes about when the writer puts us in the middle of some human action and shows it as it is illuminated and outlined by mystery. In every story there is some minor revelation which, no matter how funny the story may be, gives us a hint of the unknown, of death.

Q: What advice do you give to the college student interested in writing — especially the short story?

2. My advice is to start reading and writing and looking and listening. Pay less attention to yourself than to what is outside you and if you must write about yourself, get a good distance away and judge yourself with a stranger's eyes and a stranger's severity.

Remember that reason should always go where the imagination goes. The artist uses his reason to discover an answer in reason in everything he sees. For him, to be reasonable is to find in the object, in the situation, in the sequence, the spirit which makes it itself.

The short story writer particularly has to learn to read life in a way that includes the most possibilities--like the medieval commentators on scripture, who found three kinds of meaning in the literal level of the sacred text. If you see things in depth, you will be more liable to write them that way.

III.   THE REGIONAL WRITER

THE REGIONAL WRITER
by FLANNERY O'CONNOR

ESPRIT is privileged to publish the major portion of Miss O'Connnor's remarks on the occasion of her receiving the Georgia Writers Association's Scroll.[1]

I'm delighted to have this scroll. In fact, I'm delighted just to know that some one remembers my book two years after it was published and can get the name of it straight. I've had a hard time all

---

[1]These remarks of Flannery O'Connor were given on the occasion of her receipt of the Georgia Writers Association's Scroll. It appeared for the first time in the 1964 ESPRIT edition and presently appears in MYSTERY & MANNERS published by Farrar, Strauss & Giroux, Inc.

along with the title of that book. It's been called THE VALIANT BEAR IT ALWAYS and THE VIOLETS BLOOM AWAY, and recently a friend of mine went into a book store looking for a copy of my stories and he claims that the clerk said, "We don't have those but we have another book by that person. It's called THE BEAR THAT RAN AWAY WITH IT."

Anyway, the bear is glad to get away with one of these scrolls. I believe that for purely human reasons, and for some important literary ones too, awards are valuable in direct ratio to how near they come from home.

I remember that the last time I spoke to the Georgia Writers Association, the jist of my talk was that being a Georgia Author is a rather specious dignity, on the same order as, for the pig, being a Talmadge ham. I still think that approach has merit, particularly where there is any danger of the Georgia part of the equation over-balancing the writer part. The moral of my talk on that occasion was that a pig is a pig, no matter who puts him up. But I don't like to say the same thing twice to the same audience, and I have found, over the years, that on subjects like this, a slight shift in emphasis may produce an entirely different vision, without endangering the truth of the previous one.

The Lonely Writer

Fortunately, the Georgia writer's work often belongs in that larger and more meaningful category, Southern Literature, and it is really about that that I have a word to say. There is one myth about writers that I have always felt was particularly pernicious and untruthful — the myth of the "lonely writer," the myth that writing is a lonely occupation, involving much suffering because, supposedly, the writer exists in a state of sensitivity which cuts him off, or raises him above, or casts him below the community around him. This is a common cliché, a hangover probably from the romantic period and the idea of the artist as Sufferer and Rebel.

Probably any of the arts that are not performed in chorus line are going to come in for a certain amount of romanticizing, but it seems to me particularly bad to do this to writers and especially fiction writers, because fiction writers engage in the homeliest, and most concrete, and most unromanticizable of all arts. I suppose there have been enough genuinely lonely suffering novelists to make this seem a reasonable myth, but there is every reason to suppose that such cases are the result of less admirable qualities in these writers, qualities which have nothing to do with the vocation of writing itself.

The Writer and the Community

Unless the novelist has gone utterly out if his mind, his aim is still communication and communication suggests talking inside a community. One of the reasons Southern fiction thrives is that our best writers are able to do this. They are not alienated, they are not lonely suffering artists gasping for purer air. The Southern writer apparently feels the need of expatriation less than other writers in this country. Moreover, when he does leave and stay gone, he does so at great peril to that balance between principle and fact, between judgment and observation, which is so necessary to maintain if fiction is to be true. The isolated imagination is easily corrupted by theory, but the writer inside his community seldom has such a problem.

To call yourself a Georgia writer is certainly to declare a limitation, but one which, like all limitations, is a gateway to reality. It is a great blessing, perhaps the greatest blessing a writer can have, to find at home what others have to go elsewhere seeking. Faulkner was at home in Oxford; Miss Welty is usually "locally underfoot," as she puts it, in Jackson; Mr. Montgomery, your poetry man here, is a member of the Crawford Voluntary Fire Department, and most of you and myself, and many others are sustained in our writing by the local and the particular and the familiar without loss to our principles or our reason.

I wouldn't want to suggest that the Georgia writer has the unanimous collective ear of his community, but only that his true audience, the audience he checks himself by, is at home. There's a story about Faulkner that I like. It may be apocryphal but it's nice anyway. A local lady is supposed to have rushed up to him in a drugstore in Oxford and said, "Oh Mr. Faulkner, Mr. Faulkner, I've just bought your book! But before I read it, I want you to tell me something: do you think I'll like it?" and Faulkner is supposed to have said, "Yes, I think you'll like that book. It's trash."

It wasn't trash and she probably didn't like it, but there were others who did, and you may be sure that if there were two or three in Oxford who liked it, two or three of an honest and unpretentious bent, who relished it as they would relish a good meal, that they were an audience more desirable to Faulkner than all the critics in New York City. For no matter how favorable all the critics in New York City may be, they are an unreliable lot, as incapable as the day they were born of interpreting the Southern literature to the world.

The Southern Writer

Fortunately for the Southern writer, the Southern audience is becoming larger and more responsive to Southern writing. In the 19th century, Southern writers complained bitterly about the lack of attention they got at home, and in a good part of this century, they complained bitterly about the quality of it, for the better Southern writers were for a long time unheard of by the average Southerner. When I went to college twenty years ago, nobody mentioned any good Southern writers to me later than Joel Chandler Harris, and the ones mentioned before Harris, with the exception of Poe, were not widely known outside the region. As far as I knew, the heroes of Hawthorne and Melville and James and Crane and Hemingway were balanced on the Southern side by Brer Rabbit--an animal who can always hold up his end of the stick, in equal company, but here too much was being expected of him.

Today, every self-respecting Southern college has itself an arts festival where Southern writers can be heard and where they are actually read and commented upon, and people in general see now that the type of serious Southern writer is no longer some one who leaves and can't come home again, or some one who stays and is not quite appreciated, but some one who is a part of what he writes about and is recognized as such.

All this sounds fine, but while it has been happening, other ground has been shifting under our feet. I read some stories at one of the colleges not long ago-all by Southerners — but with the exception of one story, they might all have originated in same synthetic place that could have been anywhere or nowhere. These stories hadn't been influenced by the outside world at all, only by the television. It was a grim view of the future. And the story that was different was phony-Southern which is just as bad, if not worse, than the other, and an indication of the same basic problem.

I have a friend from Wisconsin who moved to Atlanta recently and was sold a house in the suburbs. The man who sold it to her was himself from Massachusetts and he recommended the property by saying, "You'll like this neighborhood. There's not a Southerner for two miles." At least we can still be identified when we do occur.

The present state of the South is one wherein nothing can be taken for granted, one in which our identity is obscured and in doubt. In the past, the things that have seemed to many to make us ourselves have been very obvious things, but now no amount of nostalgia can make us believe they will characterize us much longer. Prophets have already been heard to say that in twenty years there'll be no such thing as Southern literature. It will be ironical indeed if the Southern writer has discovered he can live in the South and the Southern audience has become aware of its literature just in time to discover that being Southern is relatively meaningless, and that soon there is going to be precious little difference in the end product whether you are a writer from Georgia or a writer from Hollywood, California.

The Georgia Writer

It's in these terms that the Georgia part of being a Georgia writer has some positive significance.

It is not a matter of so-called local color, it is not a matter of losing our peculiar quaintness. Southern identity is not really connected with mockingbirds and beaten biscuits and white columns any more than it is with hookworm and bare feet and muddy clay roads. Nor is it necessarily shown forth in the antics of our politicians, for the development of power obeys strange laws of its own. An identity is not to be found on the surface; it is not accessible to the poll-taker; it is not something that can become a cliché. It is not made from the mean average or the typical, but from the hidden and often the most extreme. It is not made from what passes, but from those qualities that endure, regardless of what passes, because they are related to truth. It lies very deep. In its entirety, it is known only to God, but of those who look for it, none gets so close as the artist.

The Regional Writer

The best American fiction has always been regional. The ascendancy passed roughly from New England to the Midwest to the South; it has passed to and stayed longest wherever there has been a shared past, a sense of alikeness, and the possibility of reading a small history in a universal light. In these things the South still has a degree of advantage. It is a slight degree and getting slighter, but it is a degree of kind as well as of intensity, and it is enough to feed great literature if our people — whether they be newcomers or have roots here — are enough aware of it to foster its growth in themselves.

Every serious writer will put his finger on it as a slightly different spot but in the same region of sensitivity. When Walker Percy won the National Book Award, newsmen asked him why there were so many good Southern writers and he said, "Because we lost the War." He didn't mean by that simply that a lost war makes good subject matter. What he was saying was that we have had our Fall. We have gone into the modern world with an inburnt knowledge of human limitations and with a sense of mystery which could not have developed in our first state of innocence — as it has not sufficiently developed in the rest of our country.

Not every lost war would have this effect on every society but we were doubly blessed, not only in our Fall, but in having a means to interpret it. Behind our own history, deepening it at every point, has been another history. Mencken called the South the Bible Belt, in scorn and thus in incredible innocence.

In the South we have, in however attenuated a form, a vision of Moses' face as he pulverized our idols. This knowledge is what makes the Georgia writer different from the writer from Hollywood or New York. It is the knowledge that the novelist finds in his community. When he ceases to find it there, he will cease to write, or at least he will cease to write anything enduring. The writer operates at a peculiar crossroads where time and place and eternity somehow meet. His problem is to find that location.

FINAL COMMENTS

BY
JOHN J. QUINN, S.J.

I. THE VIOLENT BEAR IT AWAY
A Review

Miss Flannery O'Connor, the Southern Writer who owns an enviable reputation as one of America's more distinguished literary artists, has added cubits to her literary stature with her new novel, *The Violent Bear It Away*.[1]

Title and Theme

The title and theme of this original story is contained in St. Matthew's text: From the days of John the Baptist until now, the Kingdom of Heaven suffers violence, and the violent bear it away. (11:12)

Since the context is concerned with Christ's commendation of

---

[1]This is an expanded version of the review that originally appeared in the March 1st, 1960 number of BEST SELLERS, the University of Scranton's semi-monthly Book Review. It is so presented to introduce *ESPRIT* readers to Miss O'Connor and the novel that occasioned her award and remarks. It is printed with the permission of Rev. R. F. Grady, S. J., Editor of BEST SELLERS.

the Baptist's prophetic work in heralding and preparing people for the Kingdom He established here, His Church, and hereafter, Heaven, the words 'violence' and 'violent' are very important. The key-word 'violent' is used by the author in the sense both St. Thomas and St. Augustine consider it: to refer to ascetics. She extends this notion to include the passion that makes ascetics, the willingness to risk and spend one's self for God on faith. This extension is endorsed by P. Benoit, O.P., Biblical scholar, in his book, *L'Evangile Selon Saint Matthiew:* It can mean the holy violence of those who monopolize the Kingdom but only at the cost of self-efacement — renunciation.

Prof. P. A. Duhamel, in the Feb., 1960 number of *The Catholic World* magazine, further elaborates the author's interpretation of 'violent' to include the imaginative insight, the intuitive rather than the quantitative view of things, the prophetic or violent view of reality: real people everywhere struggling with real emotions.

Her real people are, so claim some critics, 'poor, God-driven Southern whites — religious fanatics.' What such claims fail to discern is what the competent critic, Caroline Gordon, perceives: "Miss O'Connor's vision of modern man — a vision not limited to Southern rural humanity . . . is as victims of a rejection of the Scheme of Redemption . . . a direct gaze at human conduct . . . through the actuality of human behavior. It is a Blakean vision . . . and it has Blake's explosive honesty."

And what the special number of the London *Times Literary Supplement* on "The American Imagination" praised: ". . . a compassion so universal that it raises all her local characters to a universal scale."

To some people, anybody who believes in God and acts on the belief is a religious fanatic. This includes everybody from backwoods prophets to readers of BEST SELLERS and *ESPRIT.*

Author's Aim

Miss O'Connor has succinctly expressed the point of her writing in "The Fiction Writer and His Country" (*The Living Novel*, a Symposium edited by Granville Hicks; Macmillan Co., 1957, and, in 1962, Collier Books' paperback edition. Also, in "The Church and The Fiction Writer" (AMERICA magazine; March 30, 1957), Miss O'Connor capsulizes her principal principle:

"The Catholic writer . . . will feel life from the standpoint of the central Christian mystery, that it has, for all its horror, been found by God to be worth dying for."

Thus, her unyielding vision of reality sees everything and everybody in relation to the revitalizing, historical fact — Man's redemption by Christ.

If the Catholic writer hopes to reveal mysteries, he will have to do it by describing truthfully what he sees from where he is.

In her latest novel, as in all her fiction, Miss O'Connor's literary technique is to 'shock' her reader into reality. She must do this because the modern reader is, unfortunately, spiritually hard of hearing and myopic. Thus, she draws large and startling figures and shouts clearly to show distortions for what they are: not natural things, but ugly and repugnant distortions. This she does by using her eyes in the security of her faith, her talents in the service of Mystery as she truthfully reveals what she sees from where she is: Man and Life as they actually are sharply seared in translating into a fiction masterpiece a shocking truth, not a pious cliché.

"The Kingdom of Heaven suffers violence, and the violent bear it away."

Story Synopsis

A fourteen-year-old orphan, Francis Marion Tarwater, has lived back-country in Powderhead, Tenn., with Mason Tarwater, his great-uncle, a self-styled Prophet. The eighty-four-year-old man makes two 'prophecies': 1.) that the Lord will call Tarwater to be a prophet; and 2.) that Tarwater will baptize Bishop, five-year-old, idiot son of the old man's nephew, Rayber. The story is the opposition to and fulfillment of Tarwater's mission. At the death of his great-uncle, Tarwater goes to the city to live with his school-teacher uncle, Rayber, and his son Bishop. The deaf uncle, deserted by his wife, tries to enlighten his nephew's darkness with the teachings of modern science and psychology. Uncle Rayber never knew nephew Tarwater had to be a prophet and did not want to be one. Nephew Tarwater's friend and mentor is the Devil. Throughout the story, the Devil's voice is heard debating, in Tarwater's mind, with the force within him driving him to fulfill his mission as prophet, especially to baptize

Bishop. This latter action Tarwater performs by drowning the child! Thus, the God-driven Tarwater fulfills part of his vocation while running away from it all. In his running away, his friend the Devil becomes actualized as the man who gives him a ride back to the country. His brutal sexual assault of the drunken Tarwater sobers the defiant prophet into a realization of what it means to deny the bread of life. Disgusted, distressed, distraught Tarwater demands visible signs which literally translate his call to be a Prophet. He fires the woods surrounding his great-uncle's cabin because he wants, like Moses, to hear divine summons in the burning bush.

An Interpretation

The struggle between Tarwater and Rayber over the latter's simpleton son is only one widening wave in the whirlpool of this tragi-comic story. The strong spiritual undertow carries every character to the vortex of Tarwater's soul. He has cast "the bread of life" away; denied his mission. So has his Uncle Rayber — and for almost the same reason: the force in them — the Kingdom — suffers violence; the 'bread' tastes extraordinarily bitter. Of ordinary bitterness, they could both take a great deal. What Tarwater cannot take is the fact that Christ is more than pure spirit. He wants to hear the voice of the Lord "out of a clear and empty sky." He wants it untouched "by any human hand or breath." Any human involvement is a lowering of himself. He has a sense of the Incarnation which terrifies him. When he feels the presence of Christ through things, he quickly turns away. As for Rayber, for him to accept the force in him would mean accepting Bishop. He believes the love he has for Bishop is senseless and takes away from his human dignity. Bishop has no spiritual or intellectual potential of his own. Christianity is repulsive to Rayber because it means loving and sanctifying what is intellectually valueless. Rayber is woefully wrong — but to what extent can he be called a sinner? This is the question about modern man and Miss O'Connor does not presume to answer it. It is in his encounter with Rayber that Tarwater knows he is running away from his vocation. He has a bad conscience. He perceives Christ even in the silence. He has, in fact, the passion of the ascetic potentially. It does not make him an ascetic because he does not know anything about asceticism, but it makes him willing to wrestle with his destiny. His prototype is Jonah but there is also some Jacob in him. He himself would prefer to be Moses and speak with the Lord in the burning bush. He wants a dramatic sign of his election. But he has to recognize Christ before he sees the bush burning. Even if this burning bush is only the woods which he has set on fire himself, it is only after he has acknowledged Christ that he can see God in the woods burning. His constant friend and mentor, the Devil, is the one who shows Tarwater what it means to deny "the bread of life."

The complications, crises, and conclusion of this 'mystery' story are so realistically and artistically recorded in finely chiseled prose that the reader marvels at the marvels Miss O'Connor works. As a true literary artist, she engages her craftsmanship in her own clear and vigorous prose to tell a story illuminated by the central Christian mystery, Man's Redemption by Christ. She has created a novel of magnitude for mature readers.

II. HER STYLE

C'est le style, c'est la femme même.
a. *The Generative Finite*
"Insight Through Sight"
"The way up is the way down."
Heraclitus : 5th century B.C. Greek
Philosopher.

FLANNERY O'CONNOR
Insight Through Sight

There were two paramount literary and philosophical/theological influences in the artistic life of Flannery O'Connor. She never met either gentleman — except in his writing: the novelist Joseph Conrad and the philosopher/theologian, writer, Wm. F. Lynch, S.J., the late Jesuit editor of *THOUGHT*, Fordham University's Quarterly Review of Culture and Idea, NY (1950-1956).

I like so much as Conrad." Of Fr. Lynch, S.J., she remarked, "Fr. Lynch is one of the most learned priests in the country, I think."

While Editor of THOUGHT, Fr. Lynch wrote a series of essays on "The Literary Imagination." Later, they were compiled into a book: CHRIST and APOLLO: *The Dimensions of The Literary Imagination* (Sheed & Ward, New York, 1960).

"...images are in themselves the path to whatever the self is seeking: to insight, or beauty, or, for that matter, to God. This path is both narrow and direct; it leads, I believe, straight through our human realities, through our labor, our disappointments, our friends, our game legs, our harvests, our subjection to time. There are no shortcuts to beauty or to insight. We must go *through* the finite, the limited,the definite, omitting none of it lest we omit some of the potencies of being-in-the-flesh. . . . The finite is not itself a generality, to be encompassed in one fell swoop. Rather, it contains many shapes, and byways and cleverness and powers and diversities and persons, and we must not go too fast from the many to the one. We waste our time it we try to go around or above or under the definite; we must literally go through it. And in taking this narrow path directly, we shall be using our remembered experience of things seen and earned in a cumulative way, to create hope in the things that are not yet seen." (7)

Fr. Lynch pictures the Imagination "as following a narrow, direct path through the finite. With every plunge through, or down into, the real contours of being, the imagination also shoots up into insight, but in such a way that the plunge down *causally generates* the plunge up. This movement he diagramed thus:

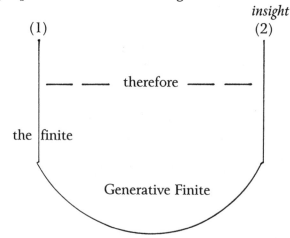

The arrival at Insight requires a basic entrance into the finite and the limited. The ancient Greek philosopher Heraclitus capsulized the method: "The way up is the way down."

A suggested, detailed "Lynch sketch" of Miss O'Connor's most anthologized story, "A Good Man Is Hard To Find," may possibly look like this:

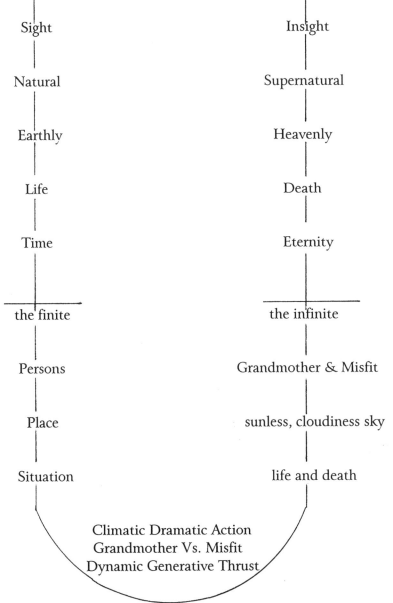

Sight	Insight
Natural	Supernatural
Earthly	Heavenly
Life	Death
Time	Eternity
the finite	the infinite
Persons	Grandmother & Misfit
Place	sunless, cloudiness sky
Situation	life and death

Climatic Dramatic Action
Grandmother Vs. Misfit
Dynamic Generative Thrust

b. *Mystery and Manners*

Flannery O'Connors'
Ars Poetica

MYSTERY and MANNERS is her ARS POETICA; Source of
Following Citations

"The first and most obvious characteristic of fiction is that it
deals with reality through what can be seen, heard, smelt, tasted, and
touched (91)."

"Fiction writing is very seldom a matter of saying things; it is
a matter of showing things (93). The meaning of a story has to be
embodied in it, has to be made concrete in it. A story is a way to say
something that can't be said any other way, and it takes every word
in the story to say what the meaning is (96). The Manicheans
separated spirit and matter. To them all material things were evil.
They sought pure spirit and tried to approach the infinite directly
without any mediation of matter. This is also pretty much the
modern spirit, and for the sensibility infected with it, fiction is hard
if not impossible *to write because fiction is so very much an incarnational
art* (68)."

"The novelist is required to create the illusion of a whole
world with believable people in it, and the chief difference between
the novelist who is an orthodox Christian and the novelist who is
merely a naturalist is that the Christian novelist lives in a larger
universe. He believes that the natural world contains the
supernatural. *And this doesn't mean that his obligation to portray the
natural is less; it means it is greater*"(175) — and her perceptive power
was ubiquitously remarkable The Catholic fiction writer is entirely
free to observe. He feels no call to take on the duties of God or to
create a new universe. He feels perfectly free to look at the one we
already have and to show exactly what he sees. He feels no need to
apologize for the ways of God to man or to avoid looking at the ways
of man to God (178).

St. Gregory wrote that every time the sacred text describes a fact, it reveals a mystery. This is what the fiction writer, on his lesser level, hopes to do. The danger for the writer who is spurred by the religious view of the world is that he will consider this to be two operations instead of one. He will try to enshrine the mystery without the fact, and there will follow a further set of separations which are inimical to art. Judgment will be separated from vision, nature from grace, and reason from imagination (184). Fiction writing is very seldom a matter of saying things; it is a matter of showing things (93).

(She quotes Conrad because she endorses him 100%):

"My task which I am trying to achieve is, by the power of the written word, to make you hear, to make you feel--it is, before all, to make you see. That--and no more, and it is everything. If I succeed, you shall find there, according to your deserts, encouragement, consolation, fear, charm, all you demand — and perhaps, also that glimpse of truth for which you have forgotten to ask (80).
    I think that for the fiction writer himself, symbols are something he uses simply as a matter of course. You might say that these are details that, while having their essential place in the literal level of the story, operate in depth as well as on the surface, increasing the story in every direction (71).
    The peculiar problem of the short-story writer is how to make the action he describes reveal as much of the mystery of existence as possible. He has only a short space to do it and he can't do it by statement. He has to do it by showing, not by saying, and by showing the concrete--so that his problem is really how to make the concrete work double time for him (98). The artist penetrates the concrete world in order to find at its depths the image of its source, the image of ultimate reality. This in no way hinders his perception of evil but rather sharpens it, for only when the natural world is seen as good does evil become intelligible as a destructive force and a necessary result of our freedom (157). If the novelist is doing what as an artist he is bound to do, he will inevitably suggest that image of ultimate reality as it can be glimpsed in some aspect of the human situation (158). But the real novelist, the one with an instinct for what he is about, knows that he cannot approach the infinite directly,

that he must penetrate the natural human world as it is. The more sacramental his theology, the more encouragement he will get from it to do just that (163). If I had to say what a "Catholic novel" is, I could only say that it is one that represents reality adequately as we see it manifested in this world of things and human relationships. Only in and by these sense experiences does the fiction writer approach a contemplative knowledge of the mystery they embody (172). . . . for the main concern of the fiction writer is with mystery as it is incarnated in human life (176)."

All these — and many others — Flannery O'Connor literary pearls are strung on Fr. Lynch's critical thread. In *Mystery and Manners* (107-114), Miss O'Connor delineates her interpretation of "A Good Man Is Hard to Find."

This story and all her fiction follow Fr. Lynch's INSIGHT through SIGHT formula. He may be the architect but she builds her own stories.

In "A Good Man..." atmosphere and character envelope her Insight through Sight and she reverses Greek Tragedy's "obscenity." Greek Tragedy never showed murder or suicide in front of the scene (*skene*); a messenger told what happened off stage (OBSCENITY). Miss O'Connor has five murders done "off stage" — behind the scenery, but her most important murder — the Grandmother — is done center stage. This would be so offensive to the Greeks as to shock them all since the subject is life and death. It is staged in Nature's Theater, the drama of life and death and life. The scene (*skene*) is a plain patch of bleak Georgia land without sun or cloud — naked nature. Beyond this setting looms large the specter of Death. Only a bullet closes the gap between a temporal paradise lost and the eternal paradise gained. This insight through sight in the entire story is a masterful usage of key transition from natural to supernatural, earth to heaven. And all this via clichés and irony (and especially comedy) on the literal level because the natural must be made credible to reach the believable of the supernatural. The Greeks would be horrified; the modern American is used to Violence. For Miss O'Connor, however, Violence is always a means, never an end. Rather, it is the catalytic agent that plunges Sight into Insight.

From the hearse — like car near the story's beginning to death of Grandmother at story's end, this somber, original story lacks joy and laughter. It is only at the end, when Insight has been reached, that the heroine, the Grandmother, now shot three times, is not the Lady but "a child and her face smiling up at the cloudless sky." (132:The Complete Stories)

"Unless you become as little children, you cannot enter The Kingdom of Heaven."

c. *Scriptural Biblical Exegesis*

Thought magazine : A Reading of Flannery O'Connor.

The analogous adaptation of scriptural exegesis to "A Good Man Is Hard To Find" can help to plumb its depths and savor its hidden meaning.

As early as 1959, Flannery O'Connor gave readers the clue to interpreting her fiction. In a symposium on the short story published by *ESPRIT*, the literary journal of the University of Scranton, she said: "The short story writer particularly has to learn to read life in a way that includes the most possibilities — like the medieval commentators on scripture, who found three kinds of meaning in the literal level of the sacred text."[2]

In his introduction to Miss O'Connor's last collection of short stories, *Everything That Rises Must Converge*, Robert Fitzgerald remarked: "Her best stories do the work that Eliot wished his plays to do, raising anagogical meaning over literal action."[3]

Since exegesis is the method to break open the rind and savor the fruit of the inner meaning, the profound depths, of the scriptures,

---

[2]Vol. III, No. 1, 10.

[3]August 18, 1994 New York: The Noonday Press, Farrar, Strauss and Giroux, 5th printing, 1966, XXX.

its analogous adaptation to an O'Connor story, "A Good Man Is Hard To Find," may well offer similar rewards. In fact, it is the operative principle that charges her two key words, Manners and Mystery.

In manners, one finds the history and ritual of a place and a people; the external, surface story and gesture that can, in her fiction, be caught in "the Southern idiom"--the very accent anchoring a history. Housed in manners is mystery. The triple dimension of mystery illuminates the context of manners. It embraces the total human condition in the crucial experience of fictional characters. It reveals spiritual insights from those material, earthly encounters that define the person.

Thus, from text and context, the referential meaning of the literal words points vertically to the three levels of meaning in the one factual level of plot. There is an endless dynamism set in motion between the surface plot level and the deeper levels of allegory, moral, and anagogy.

To translate manners and mystery into the medieval exegete's formula is to follow the distich of 14th century Nicholas of Lyre: *Littera gesta docet, quid credas allegoria, Moralis quid agas, quo tendas anagogia.*[4]

The literal teaches history, the allegorical teaches faith; The moral guides human action, the anagogical points to heaven.

The commentator on scripture used this exegetical method to uncover the richness of the sacred text. For him, scripture first gives the actual facts, the story of God's intervention in the history of humanity. This comes first and is the foundation for other meanings.

In an analogous way, the story's plot gives the concrete actual facts, the history. The words, besides giving their literal meaning, are signs of things, of realities other than themselves. Thus they yield deeper levels of meaning. To plumb the depth of an O'Connor story is to discover these richer meanings.

The doctrine, the very object of faith, the "mystery," the ensemble of truths concerning Christ and His church, Head and members of the Mystical Body, prefigured everywhere in the Old Testament and presented in the New constitute *quid credas allegoria.*

---

[4]J.P. Migne, *Patrologiae cursus completus, PL CXIII, 28.*

Hence, allegory is a belief, not a figure of speech, not a trope. This is important, for Miss O'Connor said: "Belief, in my own case anyway, is the engine that makes perception operate."[5]

Likewise, in reviewing Teilhard de Chardin's *The Phenomenon of Man*, she observed that "the poet, whose sight is essentially prophetic, will at once recognize in Teilhard a kindred intelligence. His is a scientific expression of what the poet attempts to do: penetrate matter until spirit is revealed in it. Teilhard's vision sweeps forward without detaching itself at any point from the earth."[6]

Never does her vision detach itself from the definite, finite, concrete realities of the plot. She herself saw her vocation to be true to reality.

"The novelist is required to create the illusion of a whole world with believable people in it, and the chief difference between the novelist who is an orthodox Christian and the novelist who is merely a naturalist is that the Christian novelist lives in a larger universe. He believes that the natural world contains the super-natural. And that doesn't mean that his obligation to portray the natural is less; it means it is greater" (M&M, 175). She further elucidates, "if he (the novelist) is going to show the supernatural taking place, he has nowhere to do it except on the literal level of natural events, and that if he doesn't make these natural things believable in themselves, he can't make them believable in any of their spiritual extensions" (M&M, 176).

Her realistic conclusion indicates an awareness of the difficulties inherent in such a literary method: "St. Gregory wrote that every time the sacred text describes a fact, it reveals a mystery. This is what the fiction writer, on his lesser level, hopes to do. The danger for the writer who is spurred by the religious view of the world is that he will consider this to be two operations instead of one. He will try to enshrine the mystery without the fact, and there will follow a further set of separations which are inimical to art. Judgment will

---

[5]*Mystery and Manners*, occasional prose selected and edited by Sally and Robert Fitzgerald, New York: Farrar, Straus and Giroux, 1969. Hereafter cited in text as M&M.

[6]*The American Scholar*, Autumn, 1961, Vol. 30, No. 4, 618.

be separated from vision, nature from grace, and reason from imagination" (M&M, 184).

Rooted in this last citation is her integrity as a Christian humanist. However apocalyptic her perception of our Blakean universe, it cannot be labeled myopic. On the contrary, Miss O'Connor saw "life steadily and saw it whole."

Since she believed that existence is basically unified, she needed the richly revealing method of the exegete to illuminate her vision of reality. That universal view apprehended existence in its essential unity, not in all of its diversity. Hence her integral vision artistically translated into her fascinating fiction demands that kind of critical analysis that shows a multity in unity.

A book that Miss O'Connor deeply admired and frequently mentioned is *Christ and Apollo: The Dimensions of the Literary Imagination* by William F. Lynch, S.J.[7] No doubt it helped her focus and phrase her *ars poetica, Mystery and Manners*, since most of it was written after she had read this book.

In this seminal study, Fr. Lynch explored actuality and art. Pivoted around the Incarnation, it is "an aesthetic solidly grounded upon a philosophic acceptance of man's creaturely limits in art as well as actuality."[8] This he does to achieve his purpose: "to keep literature in its rightful relation with the human and the real." His treatment of the Univocal, Equivocal, Analogical, Theological, and Christian Imagination elaborates a critical theory that undoubtedly stirred resonances in Miss O'Connor's personal and artistic temperaments.

One of Fr. Lynch's suggestions is the use of the medieval "vocabulary of the four-fold level of biblical exegesis" to refurbish our critical method of appreciating literature. Now, a dozen years later, a brilliantly penetrating study, *The Christian Humanism of Flannery O'Connor*, by David Eggenschwiler[9] complements Fr. Lynch's theory in showing how Miss O'Connor practiced it.

---

[7]New York: Sheed & Ward, 1960.

[8]Review by Charles A. Brady in *New York Times*, July 31, 1960, 4.

[9]Detroit: Wayne State University Press, 1972.

If Fr. Lynch's pioneer work can be considered a guide for Miss O'Connor, Dr. Eggenschwiler's is a conducted tour of her "country." In the former, the medieval exegete's terms are modernized: history, society, eternity.[10] The latter, in its scrutinizing the individual characters and their human situations, adopts the triple critical analysis: religious, psychological, and social perspectives of man. Such perspectives, he rightly argues, cannot be completely separated for they are merely three different contexts in which to see the same subject. For the Christian humanist, the first term, the metaphysical conception of man as a synthesis of the finite and infinite, is fundamental to any other approach. The other two terms of analysis begin with this religious conception and extend it into psychological and social contexts.[11]

The conclusion of his first chapter deserves repeating because it reveals the source of the artistic depths of her writing.

As a Christian humanist with an intense concern for art as well as for faith, she presents man in his relationships to God, to himself, and to other men, and she reveals that all of these relationships are indivisible aspects of his being. Thus, even as she shows the many ways in which man tries to destroy his essential, whole self, she also shows that those attempts can never entirely succeed; the very interrelationships of his motives indicate that the whole self cannot be completely destroyed and that man remains free enough to be healed.[12]

The moral instruction which flows from the dogma, from the mystery, mirrors the inward drama of the soul for it reflects his misery and sin as well as the destiny God calls him to as adopted son in Christ. This is represented in *moralis quid agas*, the amendment of human life and practical instruction in good Christian conduct.

The whole area of human freedom is here. Here, too, is the arena of grace. As Miss O'Connor expressed it: "The Catholic novel can't be categorized by subject matter, but only by what it assumes

---

[10]Lynch, *op. cit.*, 194.

[11]Eggenschwiler, *op. cit.*, 24.

[12]*Ibid.*, 30.

about human and divine reality. It cannot see man as determined; it cannot see him as totally depraved. It will see him as incomplete in himself, as prone to evil but as redeemable when his own efforts are assisted by grace. And it will see this grace as working through nature, but as entirely transcending it, so that a door is always open to possibility and the unexpected in the human soul. Its center of meaning will be Christ; its center of destruction will be the devil. No matter how this view of life may be fleshed out, these assumptions form its skeleton" (M&M, 196-7).

Aware that her audience did not all share this view, Miss O'Connor realistically reveals her use of violence as a literary means to achieve her artistic end: to make the reader see her vision.

"The universe of the Catholic fiction writer is one that is founded on the theological truths of the Faith, but particularly on three of them which are basic — the Fall, the Redemption, and the Judgment. These are doctrines that the modern secular world does not believe in. It does not believe in sin, or in the value that suffering can have or in eternal responsibility, and since we live in a world that since the sixteenth century has been increasingly dominated by secular thought, the Catholic writer often finds himself writing in and for a world that is unprepared and unwilling to see the meaning of life as he sees it. This means frequently that he may resort to violent literary means to get his vision across to a hostile audience, and the images and actions he creates may seem distorted and exaggerated to the Catholic mind" (M&M, 185).

Her capsulized description of grace is theologically sound and quite modern. Perhaps her reading of Henri de Lubac, S.J., encouraged her to espouse recent theological thought that sees grace as concerned with the communication of the divine life to man whereby man becomes more fully human, more truly himself, in his reception of the divine personality of Christ. Such thinking reflects a world in which Christians refuse to distinguish between the vertical spiritual life and the horizontal secular life of everyday. The final basis for such a view is the "intersection of the timeless with time," to use the words of T. S. Eliot in *Four Quartets*, which is the Incarnation.

"He (the modern reader) has the mistaken notion that a concern with grace is a concern with exalted human behavior, that it is a pretentious concern. It is, however, simply a concern with the human reaction to that which, instant by instant, gives life to the soul. It is a concern with a realization that breeds charity and with the charity that breeds action. Often the nature of grace can be made plain only by describing its absence" (M&M, 204).

Quo tendas anagogia is the eschatological sense, that of the four last things (death, judgment, heaven, hell), the celestial realities which are no longer the symbol of something else. Anagogy "concerns spiritual mysteries and ascends to the loftier and more sacred secrets of heaven."[13]

The classic, all-inclusive example is Jerusalem, which is the historical city of the Jews, the Church, the Christian soul, and the church triumphant — the heavenly Jerusalem.[14]

Anagogical meaning is "the moment of truth." It is the grace-full, free response on the part of man in his encounter with Christ in his life. That encounter is staged in the earthly, concrete realities of time and history. Its repercussions, however, echo throughout eternity. It is a physical action with spiritual dimensions. In her fiction, it may be a symbol or an image or a situation.

She herself defined anagogical as that" which had to do with the Divine life and our participation in it" (M&M, 72). This sounds so much like her understanding of grace that either the terms may be interchangeable or grace may be considered the partial, temporal participation of the divine life by man during his earthly pilgrimage and Anagogy, the victorious man's eternal fulfillment according to his individual capacity.

Another interesting observation is Miss O'Connor's grouping the three deeper levels of meaning inherent in the one surface level as "the anagogical vision" (M&M, 72).

She did not write mystery stories; she wrote stories about Mystery.

AN INTERPRETATION

---

[13]John Cassian, *Collationes*, PL XLIX, 962-5.

[14]This entire treatment is indebted to "On Early Christian Exegesis," by Walter J. Burghardt. S.J., *Theological Studies*, XI (1950), 104-6.

An intelligent analogous adaptation, not a slavish literal application of the distich, to Miss O'Connor's fiction helps the reader discern the depths of her literary artistic work. Here too Miss O'Connor is our best guide. Her remarks added as glossarial comment on the hermeneutical approach in addition to her own observations on the story under consideration (M&M, 107-114) direct our attention to her purpose and its artistic realization.

It would not be amiss to alert readers to an O'Connor story that, however neat a division offered by the medieval exegete's method of studying scripture, its application to a modern American writer's secular stories must be made cautiously.

Not only would Miss O'Connor flatly reject the elevation of her fiction to scriptural heights (which we are not doing), she would rightly resent so slavish an imposition of the exegete's method as to uncover a singular definitive interpretation of her literary art.

Literature does not work that way--nor did Miss O'Connor. Her finely chiseled prose is not so subject to finely chiseled categories as to admit a facile interpretation. Rather, this exploratory excursion into one of her stories is a measured investigation according to the central technique she herself suggested. It is a modest proposal: an application of her own dictum to find three kinds of meaning in the literal level as the medieval commentators on scripture did. It is the apposite approach which not only respects the mysteries of language and man, but also deepens the reader's reverential respect for both. Both are kept intact and the enriching experience enhances the reader's appreciation of her literary achievement.

However much a critical method--*explicatio* or exegesis--may illuminate a story--secular or sacred, it is not meant to explain it away. Medieval exegesis applied to a modern writer is a technique Miss O'Connor suggested for her own writing. It is an exciting and revealing adventure, but its limits must be recognized. She herself capsulized such limitations for reader and writer.

"The type of mind that can understand good fiction is not necessarily the educated mind, but it is at all times the kind of mind that is willing to have its sense of mystery deepened by contact with reality, and its sense of reality deepened by contact with mystery" (M&M, 79).

"This is not to say that he (the serious fiction writer) doesn't have to be concerned with adequate motivation or accurate references or a right theology; he does; but he has to be concerned with these only because the meaning of his story does not begin except at a depth where these things have been exhausted. The fiction writer presents mystery through manners, grace through nature, but when he finishes there always has to be left over that sense of Mystery which cannot be accounted for by any human formula" (M&M, 153).

As literary artist, not Christian propagandist, Miss O'Connor portrays human people in our natural world to make both believable. She has so successfully joined mystery with fact, judgment with vision, nature with grace, and reason with imagination that her "reasonable use of the unreasonable" demands violent literary means to realize her vision.

The literal level of plot is skeletally simple. The flesh and blood are contributed by the three deeper levels. According to Miss O'Connor, "this is the story of a family of six which, on its way driving to Florida, gets wiped out by an escaped convict who calls himself the Misfit. The family is made up of the Grandmother and her son, Bailey, and his children, John Wesley and June Star and the baby, and there is also the cat and the children's mother. The cat is named Pitty Sing, and the Grandmother is taking him with them, hidden in a basket" (M&M, 109).

The story spotlights the Grandmother, "the heroine of the story," and the Misfit. The setting is stark. "The road was about ten feet above (the ditch into which the overturned car threw its passengers) and they could see only the tops of the trees on the other side of it. Behind the ditch they were sitting in there were more woods, tall and dark and deep."[15]

"Behind them the line of woods gaped like a dark open mouth." (3.138)

"There was not a cloud in the sky nor any sun." (3, 141)

This setting is apposite because "It is the extreme situation that best reveals what we are essentially, and I believe there are times when writers are more interested in what we are essentially than in

---

[15]*3 by Flannery O'Connor*, New York: A Signet Book, The American Library, 1964, 136. Hereafter cited in text as 3.

the tenor of our daily lives" (M&M, 113). Her characters are "on the verge of eternity." The Grandmother "is in the most significant position life offers the Christian. She is facing death" (M&M, 110).

Against this mise-en-scene, Miss O'Connor stages her story. It pivots around the final conversation between the Grandmother and the Misfit. Its central focus is on the literal level which Miss O'Connor wanted to be taken in all its literalness to discover its spiritual extensions. It is the age-old theme of appearances vs. reality; the plunge from sight into insight.

In their words, the characters reveal their true selves. In the author's words, the story reveals the readers' selves.

The depths of the Misfit, a "prophet gone wrong" (M&M, 110), and the shallowness of a "lady," the Grandmother, are dramatically, violently revealed. Although "it's some that can live their whole life out without asking about it (the Grandmother) and it's others has to know why it is" (the Misfit) (3, 139), both have to live their choice until death rings down the curtain. To know why life is is to reach beyond man's greedy grasp of appearances to apprehend the reality behind them. This is unforgettably underscored in the conversation about Christ and His role in their times and history and lives.

The irony of this situation is enhanced by the technique of "dramatic monologue." The Misfit is not really listening to the Grandmother's missionary mutterings to pray. He is another Christ-intoxicated character from the O'Connor gallery: an alienated agnostic anguishing for belief: an isolated positivist whose horizons are his eyelids: a sadistic, self-sufficient skeptic suffering from Fundamental dyspepsia.

In the terrible truth of its literalness, the Misfit's stark summation stirs the Grandmother's stagnant Christian springs. "He (Jesus Christ) thrown everything off balance. If He did what He said, then it's nothing for you to do but throw away everything and follow Him, and if He didn't, then it's nothing for you to do but to enjoy the few minutes you got left the best way you can—by killing somebody or burning down his house or doing some other meanness to him. No pleasure but meanness" (3, 142).

When "the grandmother's head cleared for an instant," she said to the Misfit, "Why you're one of my babies. You're one of my own children!" When "she reached out and touched him on the shoulder," the Misfit shot her (3, 143).

On the level of allegory is Miss O'Connor's usual pre-occupation with the relationship of sin to redemption within human experience. She referred to her first collection, of which this is the title story, as "stories about Original Sin."[16] The citation from St. Cyril of Jerusalem (from his instruction to his catechumens), confirms the central concern of these stories in Original Sin and Redemption. As she said, "I see from the standpoint of Christian orthodoxy. This means that for me the meaning of life is centered in our Redemption by Christ and that what I see in the world I see in its relation to that" (M&M, 32).

Hence, within the human and Christian context of the story, there is both the natural brotherhood of man and the supernatural adoption into the Divine family via the Incarnation and Redemption.

Dr. Eggenschwiler's "clinical" analysis of The Misfit adds telling insights not only to an exegetical approach but a revelation to Miss O'Connor's admitted indebtedness to the Hawthorne tradition of allegory; i.e., man's relation to sin and evil.

Since the subject of the story is Original Sin and since The Misfit is the spokesman, Dr. Eggenschwiler's revelatory remarks in his "Demons and Neuroses" chapter invite summation.[17]

He describes The Misfit according to Kierkegaard's religious psychology as both "forms of the demonic man who wills to be himself in despair, the active and the passive forms."[18]

The former is "the defiant assertor of its own power and separateness"; the latter lives in spite rather than active defiance. The passive form is also a 'despair of manliness,' since the individual does will to be himself in disrelation to God. . . . The passive differs from the active form of the self in that it is concerned not with its power but with its suffering, its misery, its victimization; yet these two

---

[16]*Everything That Rises Must Converge*, XXII.

[17]*Op. cit.*, 46-52.

[18]*The Sickness Unto Death:* Princeton University Press, 1941, 107-119.

forms are complementary manifestations of the same egoism, as closely related as the paranoiac's feelings of grandeur and persecution.[19]

The words and actions of this complex but unified character, The Misfit, are artistically integrated in an economy and precision that justify Dr. Eggenschwiler's interpreting him in terms of the demonic in order to reconcile his religious and psychological interpretations. "...this approach maintains that the origins of such despair are in man's freely chosen disassociation from God but that the manifestations of the despair concern the clinical psychologist."[20]

Based on this character delineation is Dr. Eggenschwiler's suggested approach to the Misfit in terms of religious allegory. This is very significant since the story deals with Original Sin.

The patricide (The Misfit has killed his father but cannot remember doing it) then symbolizes the rebellion of the Fall; the persistent punishment for unremembered crimes suggests the condition of man in original sin; The Misfit's sense of unjustified treatment suggests man's refusal to accept his fallen and sinful state; the climactic killing of the grandmother who offers forgiveness and love symbolizes the crucifixion and the refusal of grace.[21]

"On this incident (the patricide) both the Freudian and allegorical approaches substantiate the existential reading. For the Freudian, intense anxiety develops from killing (or more usually the desire to kill) the father, since the father is loved and respected as well as hated. The amnesia which frees the Oedipal man from psychological suffering also frees the demonic man from the guilt that would refute his independence. If the demonic man is to be completely his own lord and master, he cannot admit an absolute outside of his own wishes; thus he cannot allow himself to feel guilty about what he has done, especially about the central act that has declared his independence from the father. Similarly, in terms of the Fall, man asserts himself against the power outside of himself; then

---

[19]Eggenschwiler, *op. cit.*, 50.

[20]*Ibid.*, 51.

[21]*Ibid.*, 46.

he must forget the Fall to deny guilt and to deny that there was anything to fall from."[22]

The partial allegory of the Fall in the story is an analogical rendering of The Misfit's rejection of God and his consequent estrangement. The clinical symptoms validate that estrangement through recognizable pattern of behavior.[23]

The logical and Christian consequence lead to the third level, the Moral, and the Christian conduct flowing from these beliefs. Here, too, in the main characters' inward drama of the soul is mirrored the graced or disgraced actions that humanize and Christianize or depersonalize and brutalize man--in and out of fiction.

It is on this level that the presence or absence of grace is noted in what Miss O'Connor has decided is "probably some action, some gesture of a character that is unlike any other in the story, one which indicates where the real heart of the story lies" (M&M, 111). It is the Grandmother's reaching out and touching the Misfit on the shoulder, the maternal instinct to embrace the child.

Her head clears for an instant and she realizes, even in her limited way, that she is responsible for the man before her and joined to him by ties of kinship which have their roots deep in the mystery she has been merely prattling about so far. At this point, she does the right thing, she makes the right gesture (M&M,111-112).

The redemptive moment that constitutes the grandmother's words and action is preceded and followed by violence. This is the shocking, sobering literary technique--this unique use of violence-- Miss O'Connor so effectively utilizes in all her stories. She explains why: Our age not only does not have a very sharp eye for the almost imperceptible intrusions of grace, it no longer has much feeling for the nature of the violences which precede and follow them.... in my own stories I have found that violence is strangely capable of returning my characters to reality and preparing them to accept their moment of grace. Their heads are so hard that almost nothing else

---

[22] *Ibid., 48-49*

[23]*Ibid.,* 51.

will do the work (M&M, 112).

This dramatic return to reality with all its definite concrete particularities prepares the Grandmother to accept her moment of grace. Staging such redemptive moments on the literal level of the story sets up reverberations below that level of plot to the triple levels supporting it. Together, the three deeper levels represent facets of Mystery. For the Christian humanist, Mystery is the essential man, the whole man becoming, developing his human potential and promise, struggling to complete his integrity via love.

In Miss O'Connor's integral Christian humanism, love is never an accomplished fact but always a continuing struggle. And man is never a problem to be solved but a mystery to be respected.

In the grandmother's acknowledgment and admission of kinship is rooted a twofold belief demanding a unified action. There is the kinship of all members of the human family; i.e., the solidarity of mankind and there is also the kinship in evil; i.e., the solidarity of mankind in Original Sin.

The Grandmother is brought to reality; appearances of the 'lady' are seen through for the first time in her life. In fact, it is only in death that she is called "a woman." Not only the Misfit, but she, too, has, in her own way, as the Misfit in his, refused to "throw away everything" and follow Jesus. Appearances no longer count; 'seems' is an empty word; violence—her entire family murdered—has paved the way to the right gesture. It has taken her all her life to make it. What she had always thought herself to be, a Christian lady, must now be violently reconciled to what she finds herself really to be, a selfish, self-righteous, "hypocritical old soul." She has discovered, on the very edge of eternity, that evil itself is the most humanly common thing in the world; that good is uncommon. Small wonder, "A Good Man Is Hard To Find."

So much can be said about Sin as destructive, alienating, and detachment and Grace as reconciliation, constructive atonement (at-one-ment) in this story of man's encounter with Christ. However much some people try to make the Misfit an existential hero or spokesman for the alienated agnostics of today, Miss O'Connor reveals the moral sterility of his world. The time-honored symbols of clouds and sun highlight this fact. With their Christian extensions, the sun, suggesting divinity, and the clouds, suggesting rain, a biblical symbol for grace, assume a frighteningly realistic dimension, for "there was not a cloud in the sky nor the sun" (3, 141).

The eschatological sense of anagogy is literally delineated. The story treats the four last things: death, judgment, heaven, and hell. For Miss O'Connor, however, there is no judgment in that she consigns characters eternal slots. Rather, there is for Grandmother and Misfit that self judgment that is deep in mystery—life's mystery. The grandmother does not discern it; the Misfit does not accept it. The violent climax forces them to face the religious reality. The grandmother embraces it; the Misfit, logically and temporarily, ignores it.

However, Miss O'Connor takes more latitude in Anagogy than the exegete. For her, it is that "which had to do with the Divine life and our participation in it" (M&M, 111).

In fact, in her labeling all three levels as "the anagogical vision," one cannot press too hard for neat, clear-cut divisions. The hermeneutical tool is a means to unlock the treasures of her fiction-- and one should not force the lock.

Thus, the Redemption of man by Christ is the prism through which this story is reflected in its deeper levels. The concrete details of the literal level combine to reveal the rich significance of a Christic reality: the brotherhood of man, the human family, becomes Sonship by divine adoption, and all are children of Our Father in heaven. In this story, Miss O'Connor takes this truth to its Christic conclusion: the children go home to God, their Father. This remarkable achievement is wrought in words. It is as literary artist that Miss O'Connor fulfilled her vocation and enriched our literary tradition.

In a verbal economy that is stunning in scope and effect, she shows us the grandmother's triumph: the grandmother who half sat and half lay in a puddle of blood with her legs crossed under her like a child's and her face smiling up at the cloudless sky (3, 143).

However sketchily this experimental reading of a Flannery O'Connor story according to the exegetical method, it hopefully serves as a technique for garnering a rich harvest. It is suggested because she herself suggested it. It is no substitute for the experience of reading the story itself. She said: "A story really isn't any good unless it successfully resists paraphrase, unless it hangs on and expands in the mind. Properly, you analyze to enjoy, but it's equally true that to analyze with any discrimination, you have to have enjoyed already" (M&M,108).

The literal level of this story is a family trip. It becomes a trip through time to eternity after it takes a providential detour. It encircles Christ, the center of man's life, and, literally, shoots off in a different direction. Instead of reaching Florida, fabled country of eternal youth, the Grandmother (and family) reach eternity. In this detour, the significance of Christ to each individual (and society) is spelt out. Ironically, it is the Misfit who stresses the mystery of Christ's role in man's life: and he does—and does not know — the full import of his words.

In the Grandmother, the presence of Christ is interiorized in her soul. She--representing herself, family, and society--grasps the truth of Christ for the first time in her life.

She says and does the right thing, makes the right gesture. She reaches out to touch her 'son'--the Misfit's wearing her son Bailey's shirt confirms this identity. Her action has Christic dimensions: it is the moral "ought" of translating divine mystery into human fact.

This would have to be an action or gesture which was both totally right and totally unexpected; it would have to be one that was both in character and beyond character; it would have to suggest both the world and eternity. The action or gesture I'm talking about would have to be on the anagogical level, that is, the level which has to do with the Divine life and our participation in it. It would be a gesture that transcended any neat allegory that might have been intended or any pat moral categories a reader could make. It would be a gesture which somehow made contact with mystery (M&M, 111).

In this and all her stories, Miss O'Connor has presented mystery through manners, grace through nature, judgment joined to vision, reason linked with imagination, but when she finishes "there always has to be left over that sense of Mystery which cannot be accounted for by any human formula" (M&M, 153).

From the surface level of plot to the depths of anagogic richness, the realm of mystery, is the path pursued by a hermeneutical approach to her sacramental vision of modern man. The constant interaction of all four levels gives her fiction its coherent integrity, its dynamism, and its singular prophetic vision. Like Dante, she has shown us the depth and height of our human aspirations in the tragicomic vision of her fiction.

Reprinted by permission from THOUGHT, Fordham University Quarterly Vol. XLVIII, No. 191, Winter 1973.

INDEX